In a Quiet Place

A devotional of prophetic poetry,
pointing to the Word of God

DAVID COCKING

Published by Impressum, NSW Australia
www.impressum.com.au

ISBN: 978-1-922588-17-3 (paperback) | 978-1-922588-18-0 (ebook)

NATIONAL LIBRARY OF AUSTRALIA
A catalogue record for this work is available from the National Library of Australia

Cover design by Impressum
Text © David Cocking
Production layout by Impressum
Printed on demand by Ingram Group

PREFACE

2 Corinthians 3:3-4

And I wrote this very thing for you, lest, when I came, I should have sorrow over those from whom I ought to have joy, having a confidence in you all that my joy is the joy of you all. For out of much affliction and anguish of heart I wrote to you, with many tears, not that you should be grieved, but that you might know the love which I have so abundantly for you.

2 Corinthians 3:6-8

Who also made us sufficient as ministers of the new covenant, not of the letter but of the Spirit; for the letter kills, but the Spirit gives life.

2 Corinthians 3:16-18

Nevertheless when one turns to the Lord, the veil is taken away. Now the Lord is the Spirit; and where the Spirit of the Lord is there is liberty. But we all, with unveiled face, beholding as in a mirror the glory of the Lord, are being transformed into the same image from glory, just as by the Spirit of the Lord.

John 17:22-24

And the glory which You gave Me I have given them, that they may be one, and that the world may know that You have sent Me, and have loved them as You have loved Me. "Father, I desire that they also whom You gave Me may be with Me where

I am, that they may behold My glory which You have given Me; for You loved Me before the foundation of the world.

JOHN 1:1-3

In the beginning was the Word, and the Word was with God, and the Word was God. He was in the beginning with God. All things were made through Him, and without Him nothing was made that was made.

How do I hear from God and how do I know it is Him? Will He speak to me? Does He even know who I am?

These are common questions I often hear when talking to people searching for answers to life's problems. And let's face it, we all have those problems we wish we could resolve in an instant. For over twenty years I have worked in the Construction Industry, solving and sometimes causing problems when a solution did not at first present itself. As my Christian walk progressed I realized that God was wanting to talk to me about many topics surrounding my life and the lives of those people I would come into contact with. As He began to speak to me I began to see solutions where they had not been possible previously. As my trust grew I began to lean more and more on Him for answers, noticing that he wanted to talk with me all the time. I on the other hand, did not always want to talk with him. Life's distractions allowed me to hear from God less and less. After a while I realized that all my solutions would come after I had spent time reading scripture and sitting in a quiet place waiting to hear from my Father. In time I found that I wanted to hear more and more from my Father in Heaven and decided to write down what he was saying to me so that I could reflect on his advice. After a while I would start to write things down and think of someone specific that God was wanting me to speak to on His behalf. I would feel a heaviness on my heart that would not go until I had written exactly what the Lord had told me to write and issued it to the person I had been thinking about. As my faith in the accuracy of the content increased, so did the personal nature of the written conversations between God and the person God was using me to write to. The joy seen on people's faces when they have tangible evidence that our Father in Heaven knows them, loves them, sees them emotionally and provides them with very specific details surrounding their current heartache is living proof He exists, and is a pure joy to be part of.

As I began to show other people the texts (with names removed), I could see the words lift off the page into the reader's heart. At that moment, I began to realise that other people could benefit from the anointed words and not just the specific recipient. As one reader described it, "The words were like a balm washing over my soul".

From this experience the Lord showed me that he wanted His words to be spoken to many souls, regardless of race or gender, and so the idea of this book was born.

It has been broken into categories that I like to call moments. We all have them and we all want them, but we do not always know what the difference is. It is my intention that after you have read this book, you will have established your own quiet place to go to and spend time with God developing your intimacy with your Heavenly Father. As this intimacy grows you will then be ready to hear and understand what He wants to say to you—about you and your life and those around you. Just like one situation where a person's heart was broken through one of life's trials. Before going to bed they were deeply upset and had many questions to put to God. During the night God spoke through me to give clear and specific reassurance that he was indeed in the middle of the situation and provided love and reassurance to the reader. The words and scripture given were so specific to the reader that they could not provide any other explanation for me being able to quote the scripture by which they lived their life. When problems arise you to will be able to receive and understand Heaven's solutions providing insight and love to those in need, including yourself.

I would like to thank my wife Michelle for all of her love and support. You have been and always will be my rock, bringing the best out of me to succeed when I have nothing left. To my children Torren and Serena, thankyou for showing me the fun in life. A smile and a cuddle solve many things. Thank you to my pastors, Marty and Elly Webb, for their theological and prophetic insights and to my brothers and sisters in Christ who have always had my back.

FOREWARD

David has put together a collection of poems that have a unique tone to them. A tone that carries healing, encouragement and a gentle sound of God's voice to comfort and console the heart. When you read each verse it presents possibilities for personal revelation directed to an area of need or desire. I'm sure this collection will take its own journey into the lives of those who chose to read and digest its timely truth and heartfelt language. Each poem will serve as a devotional tool, and a source of prayerful reflection imparting grace in a timely manner. I'm sure many hearts will be opened to the wonder and awe of the Father's love.

Ps Martyn Webb
C3 Spectrum church
Port Stephens NSW

With a deep desire to see the word of God implanted and bring healing to a generation in need, Dave's poetic writings are a treasure to be stored in the heart of every reader.

Aimee-Louise Rewai
Dip. Christian Counselling, Prayer Minister, Celebrant

This is a collection of personal conversations spanning years, documenting David's own journey into an ever deepening and intimate friendship with the Lord. Each download contains new nuggets of revelation. David processes the Lord's daily work in his own heart, in a vulnerable and honest way through poetry, downloads, scripture and sometimes prophetic art. I pray that reading this book will also inspire you to document your own journey and friendship with the Lord as you pursue Him. -

Michelle Sansom-Sherwill
Friend, Teacher, Fellow Journal-er and God lover

Contents

Heaven's Law

Leviticus 10:2

So fire went out from the Lord and devoured them, and they died before the Lord. And Moses said to Aaron,
'This is what the Lord spoke, saying:
"By those who come near me
I must be regarded as holy;
And before all the people
I must be glorified".'

Heaven's door seen before
In the eyes of the innocent child
Set aside, no more pride
The soul is free from sin.
So take My hand, step on in,
Let your soul awakening begin.

I have no fear, I have no death,
I pour out love and free the captive soul.
I love the unjust, I love the just
I hate sin, I hate deceit,
It is a distraction to Me.
All are children to Me.

I want to help, I call them home
But free will allows man to be alone.
Alone in his darkness, free to sin
And here My work continues

I must start again.
Restore the lost, heal the sick,
Setting the captives free.
I work in all things to bring redemption
I turn the hardest heart.
But woe to those who cannot stay
They turn their hearts away.
For they are lost, they are misguided
They do not hear My voice.

I call them home, I sing to their hearts,
I reach out My hand when they are torn apart.
I pick them up, I cover them over
Released from chains within.
But still they fight, still they run,
There is nowhere to hide.

And so we begin again, how to devour pride.
Love is the answer, love is key,
It unlocks your heart to connect with Me.
Compassion for man, no matter the cost,
Not one soul would ever be lost.
For yon speak the truth, speak in love
Representing your Father in Heaven above.

Called to speak, called to teach.
1000's of souls ordained to reach.
Stretch out your hand, open your heart
On this day your ministry will start.
Help those in need, cast the seed,
Watch My mustard seeds grow.

You will not be shamed, you will not
be forgotten
For as My child who was begotten
I will stand, I will talk, side by side we
must walk.
Keeping the heat so rich in love
Representing Me, your Father above.
Take My hand and walk outside
Speak My words far and wide.

Open the hearts and souls of man
Back at the cross where it all began
Persecuted for love, hate exchanged.
Beauty for ashes, God ordained.
I will have My land restored
Heaven and earth they are the Lord's.

Be bold, be brave, speak your heart.
Redeemed and sanctified at the start,
A place to move forward from.
Walk in the light.
Pray to Me and watch the fight.

For battles are lost and won in prayer.
Learn the language, be an heir.
Inherited blessings and spiritual gifts
Freely given to love one another,
Freely given to love, brother to mother.

All can heal, all can be redeemed,
Confess your sins and seek My face.

I am here waiting in this space.
Ready to accept you no matter the sin,
Confession of guilt is where to begin.

For all are guilty, all have sinned,
But Jesus died so you would be free.
Free of sin, restored to Me.
Confess your soul and watch Me move in.
Invitation only, then we begin.
Remove the stone you have for a heart.
Replaced with My love, set apart.

Free to love, free to bless,
Open your mouth, start to confess.
Jesus is my Lord and Saviour
Come into my heart, change my behaviour.
Forgive me of my sins I have done.
I know you died on the cross for me.
Three days later you rose in victory.
Now I walk as your servant forever.
Jesus Christ my Lord and Saviour.

Romans 10:9

That if you confess with your mouth the Lord Jesus and Believe in your heart that God has raised Him from the dead, you will be saved.

Romans 10: 21

All day long I have stretched out My hands
To a disobedient and contrary people.

Simple Man

John 17:1-5

Jesus spoke these words, lifted up His eyes to heaven and said, 'Father, the hour has come. Glorify Your Son, that Your Son also may glorify You, as You have given Him authority over all flesh, that He should give eternal life to as many as You have given Him. And this is eternal life, that they may know You, the only true God, and Jesus Christ whom You have sent. I have glorified You on earth. I have finished the work which You have given Me to do. And now, O Father, glorify Me together with Yourself, with the glory which I had with You before the world was.

As I walk through the clouds, people
standing by,
I look up to the heavens, to touch the sky.
To the one who loves me, beyond all things,
Carrying me along, on his angel's wings.

I cannot see Him, touch His hand,
I walk in faith, into the promised land.
Healed, redeemed, a victorious bride,
He knows my thoughts, I have nothing to hide.

I wear my heart on my sleeve,
I hold nothing back.
He gives unconditionally, through Him I will
not lack.

For His love abounds, with an
outstretched hand.
Unconditional love, for a simple man.

Do not fear, do not cause strife,
We are all created equal, a man and wife.
Unconditional love, through all the seasons,
Ten thousand angels, ten thousand reasons.
To walk in unity, love abounding,
Peace in our hearts, angels' chorus resounding.

I wear my heart on my sleeve,
I hold nothing back.
He gives unconditionally, through Christ I
won't lack.
For His love abounds, with an
outstretched hand,
Unconditional love for a simple man.

Though my heart may ache, and my eyes
don't see,
All the love surrounding me.
I will push on, through the valleys, low,
Walking in faith, how and why I don't know.
But I do know this, I am loved and protected.
Though man may fail, Christ's love
never rejected.

Bought for a price, we could not pay,
He will light our path, lead your way.

I wear my heart on my sleeve,
I hold nothing back.
He gives unconditionally, through Christ I won't lack.
For His love abounds, with an outstretched hand,
Unconditional love for a simple man.

To eternal love, everlasting,
Our hearts renewed in righteousness.
Spirit filled, spirit led,
In Christ renewed, the old is dead.

I wear my heart on my sleeve,
I hold nothing back.
He gives unconditionally, through Christ I won't lack.
For His love abounds, with an outstretched hand,
Unconditional love for a simple man.

Jeremiah 29:11-14

For I know the thoughts that I think toward you, says the Lord, thoughts of peace and not of evil, to give you a future and a hope. Then you will call upon Me and go and pray to Me, and I will listen to you. And you will seek Me and find Me, when you search for Me with all your heart. I will be found by you, says the Lord, and I will gather you from all the nations and from all the places where I have driven you, says the Lord, and I will bring you to the place from which I cause you to be carried away captive.

The Father's Love

Habakkuk 3:11

The sun and moon stood still in their habitation; At the light of Your arrows they went,
At the shinning of Your glittering spear.

At the light of Your arrows they went,
At the shinning of Your glittering spear.
Your eyes no man can understand
In You we shall not fear.
The mountains may be standing,
The valleys may be deep.
But on Your Word we hold fast,
Your promises You keep.

Of hope and restoration,
Deliverance and freedom found.
The angels sing your praises,
A heavenly adoring sound.
That speaks to the Father lovingly,
A spring bursting in our hearts.
An outpouring of love to others
Rivers of life flow through us,
Joined in love as brothers.

Be still, be strong and loving,
Knowing I AM is He.
For on my rock you build My church,
And all I promise thee.

Will come to pass in splendor
A vision true and right.
That shows mankind My righteousness,
As sure as day follows night.

Lift up, be strong and generous,
With love toward mankind.
For in the depths of despair
True love and meaning you find.
That Jesus came to be love,
To show you how much I care.
For each tear drop is noticed, in the
heavenly sphere.

The angels walk from up above, waiting for
the moment,
Where hearts are opened freely,
To a victorious loving Father,
Who waits to enter in.
Each circumstance unique,
To overcome their sin.
So that mankind would be forgiven,
And Heaven enter in.
Victorious, clothed in righteousness,
Forgiven, loved and cherished.
Each heart saved for eternity,
Wiped clean of all human blemish.

So sing out with your praises,
Those who know My love,
And help the lost and lonely.

With prayers sent up above.
To the heavenly realm, angels watch,
And wait to enter in,
Your personal battle or circumstance,
Through love they surely win.
For each battle is a moment,
In a life of many trials.
But the true battle has been won.
Victorious He is seated high.
At the right hand side of the Father, ready to step in.
To your personal circumstance, with a prayer He will begin.

To overturn all challenges,
To work them all for good.
For those who love the Father,
His ways no one understood.
So fear not, My beloved people,
I will not leave or forsake you.
For My love to you is never ending,
To see you victorious, in the life I give.

To see you love mankind,
As you have seen My son rises.
From the grave to life for eternity,
He overcame the earth.
With all its sin and proudness,
Baseless without worth.
But now My Son lives upon high,
In Heaven's glory seated.

Death and sin forever, they have been defeated,
So stand firm in My promise,
Redemption, resurrection, loving
kingdom, wholeness.
Open your heart to the Father
His wholeness knows no end.
A Savior's promise, truth and love,
In your heart He will mend.

Make new and give you a life of truth,
Full of love and blessing.
It starts with a single declaration,
A simple confession.
That Jesus is our Lord and Savior,
Taken to the cross.
Where He died and rose three days later,
Our sins were all forgiven.
Now seated high at the right hand side of
the Father,
Jesus, He has risen.

A Savior's story, a Savior's promise of life
in abundance.

John 10:10

The thief comes only to steal and kill and destroy; I came that they may have life, and have it abundantly.

Matthew 6:33

But seek first His kingdom and His righteousness, and all these things will be added to you.

Psalm 16:11

You will make known to me the path of life; In Your presence is fullness of joy; In Your right hand there are pleasures forever.

God Redeems

Yan-a-man-a-saw

It is a clean slate given to people who have a deep regret and are spiritually damaged people.

Pierced heart as Jesus was pierced
Isolated as Christ was isolated
Rejected as Christ was rejected
Abandoned as Christ was abandoned
Naked as Christ was naked
No human would console him
Total failure as a human
To feel total oppression
God redeems
You experience true redemption, that nothing can save you. Nowhere to hide. Nothing to trade with. You are totally at the mercy of God through Jesus Christ.

It is the miracle of salvation.
Tell all who are bound how to find freedom through Jesus Christ.

I am the truth the way the light. No-one can get to the Father except through me, Jesus Christ.

Matthew 4:16

The people who sat in darkness have seen a great light,
And upon those who sat in the region and shadow of death.
Light has dawned.

The Refuge

Numbers 26:65

They shall surely die in the wilderness.
These are those who were numbered by

Leaders must know what resources they have before they develop their plans and design their strategies.

Where do you go when you have nowhere
to go?
What do you see when you are blinded by
your circumstance?
Who will care when loved ones are no more?
Who will provide shelter when your home is
no more?
These are those who cannot speak.
Broken, wounded heartfelt shame,
Lost, lonely, they feel the blame.

Condemnation, broken hearted,
Despair, depreciation, broken-spirited.
These are those who are numbered.

To be born again, risen up, created,
A new voice, a new heart, hope restored.
Courageous, beautiful, Heaven-sent, adorned.
Draped in the robes of righteousness, truth,
Inner man, Inner woman, Inner youth.
Glorified, sanctified, love abound,

Beauty from ashes, in Him we are found.
Cleansed through love, a holy exchange.
Washed with His blood, all sin is forgiven,
Beauty from ashes, He is risen.
To strengthen all who ask through love,
The Father watches from Heaven above.
Each one a child, He will not forsake,
Each one created in His image.

Rise up, protect and help those in need,
I have given you resources, now water the seed.
Tend to the crop, in all its seasons,
Each one is special, each one a reason.
To restore and gather up, to build a new,
Just like each new born child, just like you.

Do not lose heart, do not fear,
The Lord your God is ever present, ever near.
To guide your steps, and march on forwards,
Battle cry victorious, overcomers.

I will bring those things to pass.
I will show you My power, ever last.
I will restore those lost and broken,
For each is My child, each one is chosen.

For such a time, to bring to pass,
To glorify God who is ever last.

Go out, go forward, do not look back,
Jesus Christ will be with you, this is a pact.
A covenant blessing upon your life,
A covenant blessing between you and your wife.
Of joys to come and mercy to give,
For such a time as this, both go out and live.
Representing Jesus in all you do,
For Christ is with you now and evermore.
God bless you both and may you find
peace in all you do, together as a couple,
strengthened, united.

God's Promise – The Rainbow

Waking up with a fuzzy head my body wanted
to stay in bed,
I was not ready to face the day,
I was not ready to hear the Almighty say;
"Arise, wake up, the time is now,
I want to talk, show you how,
I want to give you information,
I want to have a conversation."

So out I get and walk on through,
Tired and sleepy, what to do.
What to say, what to pray,
How can he communicate with me this way?
I do not hear, I do not feel,
Is this guidance really real?
I'm too tired, I'm too sleepy,
God's communication is so easy.

Arise early, arise well,
God will speak to you, God will tell,
Tell you great mysteries old and new,
Revelation just for you.
As I sleep, as I slumber
God reveals, look out the window.
From vacant skies far and wide,
I cannot believe what I see, my eyes.
Glorious rainbow, fully formed,
Exact location – in the storm.

God revealed His almighty power,
God revealed His majesty.
Where you see lack, I see challenge.
Your mind does not see what I know.
In absence and darkness I see light.
This has always been the eternal fight.
In your need, I see supply,
In your wait, I see growth.
In your hurting I see love,
This is My promise from above.
A reminder of what I said I would do,
A reminder of My love for you.

I never left, I never went.
I gave My son, so that you would repent.
Walk with Me and see My hand,
Bless your lack, bless your land.
My help is here, for all to see,
My help is here, He is Me.

The Holy Spirit, ever present.
The Holy Spirit, ever near,
He brings hope out of fear.
He brings joy out of despair,
Follow His guidance to repair.

All that was lost, all that was broken,
Heaven's grace is now open.
Poured out, pressed down, abundantly given,
Proclaim the gospel – He is risen.
To give new life where it has been taken,

To give you love, pressed down, shaken.
Rejoice, sing out He is risen.
Rejoice, sing out He is here.
Loved, challenged, transformed, renewed.
The promise of Jesus Christ, in Him we
are renewed.

Genesis 9:12-17

God said "This is the sign of the covenant which I am making between Me and you and every living creature that is with you, for all successive generations; I set My bow in the cloud and it shall be for a sign of a covenant between Me and the earth, It shall come about; when I bring a cloud over the earth, that the bow will be seen in the cloud and I will remember My covenant, which is between Me and you and every living creature of all the flesh; and never again shall the water become a flood to destroy all flesh."

Ezekiel 1:28

Like the appearance of a rainbow in a cloud on a rainy day, so was the appearance of the brightness all around it. This was the appearance of the likeness of the glory of the Lord. *So when I saw it, I fell on my face, and I heard a voice of One speaking.*

Revelation 4:3

And He who sat there was like a jasper and a sardius stone in appearance; and there was a rainbow around the throne, in appearance like an emerald.

Revelation 10:1

I saw still another mighty angel coming down from heaven, clothed with a cloud. And a rainbow was on his head, his face was like the sun, and his feet like pillars of fire.

Standing In The Cold

Ephesians 6:2-4

"Honor your father and mother," which is the first commandment with promise: "That it may be well with you and you may live long on the earth."
And you, fathers, do not provoke your children to wrath, but bring them up in the training and admonition of the Lord.

Hope – The promise of things yet unseen.

Romans 8:24-25

For we are saved in this hope, but hope that is seen is not hope: for why does one still hope for what he sees? But if we hope for what we do not see, we eagerly wait for it with perseverance.

Romans 15:4

For whatever things were written before were written for our learning, that we through the patience and comfort of the scriptures might have hope.

Romans 15:13

Now may the God of hope fill you with all joy and peace in believing, that you may abound I hope by the power of the Holy Spirit.

Standing in the cold,
Bones and skin feel old.

The vision is hidden by the clouds.
The heart is faint, emotions high,
You have nothing left, but to look to the sky.

I see your pain, I see your lack,
I understand, there's no turning back.
I promised you abundance, I promised you
a home,
I promised you a life change, a journey of love.
My promises I keep, the words I speak,
They do not return to Me void.

I work in the unseen, I work in the heavenlies,
I work all day and night.
I work inside you and your wife,
Together you should not fight.
But support and nurture each other,
Open your hearts and see,
The gifts I gave each of you, are to glorify Me.

For Jesus died and paid the price,
To bring redemption to all.
And I have given you skills and promises,
To answer a generation's call.
Who will love the children?
Who will guide them home?
Who will raise up leaders,
To make the gospel known?

I have given you a message,
I have given you a voice.

I have blessed you with many things.
And now you must make a choice,
For the path is long and narrow.
It does not appeal to all.
But those who walk it find blessings,
As you answer My call.

I bestowed a gift in each of you,
To honor and obey.
To love each other unconditionally,
Despite what each might say.
For words cut deep and penetrate,
They wound the precious heart,
And left unattended, destroy,
Hope built from the start.

I saved you from the ashes,
To build a new fire within,
I saved you for a purpose,
Destroyed the curse of sin.
Grow in love, grow in grace,
Hold on to the promises spoken.
Keep and study My Word,
My promises are never broken.

Declare My love, declare My promise,
And watch My power grow.
I will move your mountain,
I will truly show,
That all things work together,
For those who love Me.

All things will be overcome,
That is My promise to thee.

Go back to what I told you,
Go back to what I said.
Go back to the words I gave you,
Don't let your hope be dead.
For hope is the source of dreams,
Visions and goals and joy.
Hope I give in abundance,
Sing it loud with all joy.

Psalm 46:10

Be still and know that I am God; I will be exalted among the nations, I will be exalted in the earth.

The Holy Spirit Introduction

Romans 8:26 NKJV

Likewise the Spirit also helps in our weaknesses. For we do not know what we should pray for as we ought, but the Spirit Himself makes intercession for us with groaning which cannot be uttered.

John14:27 NKJV

Peace I leave with you, My peace I give to you; not as the world gives do I give to you. Let not your heart be troubled, neither let it be afraid.

When you wake up in the morning,
And you have a fuzzy head;
When you go to bed in the evening
And you can't remember what you said,
Lift your heart, and talk to me,
I hear your every word.
Lift up and speak aloud to me, as the song sings from the bird.

I created you for joy,
I created you a child so precious,
Too precious to be a toy.
You have dreams, you have a purpose,
I know you know My love.
I created you so beautiful,
With peace just like the dove.

I want you to know My love,
To feel it when you walk,
I want you to know My love
To feel it when we talk
Hold My hand and walk with Me
Just like I do with mum & dad.
Take my hand and walk with Me
There's no need to feel sad.

I love you, and I care for you,
I created you a friend.
His name is the Holy Spirit,
He's with you until the end.
I'll help you learn to talk to Him
To give Him all your woes.
I'll help you to grow old with Him
To battle all your foes.

He comes in love, He comes in peace,
He wants to know your heart.
He comes as love, He comes as peace,
To bring a new-found start.
To guide you on your journey,
To give you hope renewed.
To give you knowledge and wisdom,
Uplift you when you're subdued.

I help your mother and father,
And now I'm helping you.
I help all those who need Me
Whose hearts have been renewed.

I'll lift you up, I'll carry you
To wonders never seen.
I'll show you the power of Jesus
In Him you are redeemed.

So let us take this journey
To where God wants you to be.
Let's step out in childlike faith,
Together you and Me.
I don't replace your parents
For they are a gift from God,
I help you and I help them,
Eternal from above.

So be blessed and look upon this
As a wonderful new day.
Look at Me as your new best
As someone with whom you can pray.
Don't worry or feel embarrassed
I come only in love.
A gift from your Heavenly Father
A gift from up above.

A gift of joy, a gift of peace
To help you on your way.
A gift of love everlasting,
A gift received today.
A joy, a peace, a new found love,
A gift you don't have to share
A gift that covers you day and night
Just like the clothes you wear.

A gift of very gentle love, of peace
forever more,
For you are a child of God, a child whom
I adore.
God bless you, I love you so much more.
I love you for all eternity, You I truly adore.

Your Heavenly Father
My Son Jesus Christ
My Holy Spirit.

2 Timothy 1:7 NKJV

For God has not given us a spirit of fear, but of power and of love and of a sound mind.

Amen

Glass Angel

Isaiah 63:7-9

I will mention the loving kindness of the Lord
And the praises of the Lord.
According to all that the Lord has bestowed on us,
And the great goodness toward the house of Israel,
Which He has bestowed on them according to His mercies,
According to the multitude of His loving kindness.
For He said, "Surely they are My people. Children who will not lie."
So He became their Saviour.
In all their affliction He was afflicted,
And the Angel of His presence saved them;
In His love and in His pity He redeemed them,
And He bore them and carried them All the days of old.

Glass is made from applying heat and pressure to sand. In its purest form it still has imperfections, yet those imperfections are used to give the final form its character. And so consider the number of thoughts I have for you that outnumber the plans you may have. I have given so much more thought into you and your life than you could imagine.

Psalm 139:17-18

How precious also are Your thoughts to me, O God!
How great is the sum of them!

If I should count them, they would be more in number than the sand;
When I awake, I am still with you.

Your heart is pure, and so My love, My light is able to shine through you like a glass Angel. What I placed inside you shines out from within. It is love, it is light, it is Jesus Christ. As a lighthouse must be securely anchored on the rock to warn others of impending danger if they don't change course, so too does My Word, spoken through you. You are anchored in the Word, on solid rock. The light of your house shines through the darkest storms to those in need. Your glass is pure and clean. There is no covering over your glass. The vision I give to others through you is never distorted or held back. I acknowledge your faith and dedication through My Word to give you edification.

Your heart is pure
Your sight is clean
The powers you fight are unseen.
But in the dark, you can see,
The light I give, I give to thee.

For you stand strong, in the darkest hour,
You stand for truth in our Saviour's power.
The truth, the light, the way ahead,
Is Jesus's love, the words He said.

For in the day when all is given
Mankind will see Christ is risen.
He will show the love inside,
He will breakdown the strongholds, far
and wide.
He will hold the power to Heaven,
For Jesus Christ, He is risen.

You speak My words to all mankind
You give My love to the darkest mind.
You lift people up when they are low,
You guide their hearts, show where to go.
You remain pure when others fade,
You remain strong in the darkest day.
You remain courageous when times are hard,
You remain My child throughout the storm.

I lift you up when you feel weak,
I give you the words, when you do not speak.
I feel your pain when others cannot,
I hear your cries when others have forgot.
But do not despair for I am here,
Do not despair, I am near.
We walk in love forever more,
We walk in peace across the land
We walk together hand in hand.

I draw near to you, and you to me,
This is relationship as it should be.
This is the power of My Holy Spirit,
This is the calling on your life.

This is a letter from Me to you,
This is our relationship, through and through.

I bring you peace, love and health,
I bring you knowledge, sustain your wealth.
Of riches aplenty, Heaven abound,
For in you no blemish I have found.
Restored and sanctified by Jesus on the cross,
I walk with you to pray for the lost.
The broken, the hurt, the undelivered,
Your life a testimony to be preached
For through your life many will be reached.
So continue on, step out in faith,
Together we will reach out to the human race.
To speak the gospel far and wide,
Into the darkness, nowhere to hide.
For through you I speak, and in you I see,
The love of Jesus, the love for Me.
The love of My Word, the love outpoured,
My glass angel, you are adored.
Blessed are you and your family for many generations to come.

What is the colour of your heart?

Proverbs 4:23

Keep your heart with all diligence,
For out of it spring the issues of life.

Spring – physical bounce
Spring – non-stop source
Heart – inner core = spirit/soul
Physical = life

Proverbs 4:25

Let your eyes look straight ahead,
And your eyelids look right before you.
Ponder the path of your feet,
And let all your ways be established

A heart is grown, a heart is sown,
The inner life in thee.
Your heart is strong, your heart is weak,
You think I cannot see.
I prepared you in the quiet times,
In heaven far above.
I created you a triune being,
A being made of love.

The love I gave, I gave freely,

The love I show, I show to thee.
It never ends or finishes.
The love I have, it builds you up,
It never ever diminishes.
For you were made and you were paid for,
A ransom that was due.
The price He paid, the pain endured,
Jesus endured it for you.

To give you a life, to give you peace,
To create in you a new heart.
To give you joy, to give you love,
To give you a clean start.
Washed in love, washed in grace,
It's freedom undefined.
To fool the clever, to confuse the proud,
The power of love renowned.

I love you child with all your mess,
I love you more each day.
I love you child when you confess,
The thoughts you cannot say.
I hear your heart, I see your mind,
It really is ok.
I listen out for My Word spoken,
At the beginning of the day.

I search the land, I search man's hearts,
I know what is inside.
There is no place to run to,
From me you cannot hide.

I search you because I love you,
I want to heal your heart.
I search you because I care for you,
To give you a fresh start.

So come to Me, all who are weary,
Come to Me and rest.
Come to Me, lay your burdens down,
Release them from your chest.
Open up, let it out, you cannot carry it all,
Release your heavy burdens to Me,
And then stand up tall.

Rejoice in Me, rejoice I say,
For in you I am working.
To cleanse your heart of darkness,
And replace with a beautiful love.
A love that heals, a love that cares,
A love that sets you free.
A love that covers a multitude of sins,
A perfect love in Me.

I want your pain, I want your hurt,
It was never yours to carry.
It was not yours to hold on to,
So quickly, do not tarry.

Release your heart, release your soul,
And watch what I will do.
The love of Jesus washes clean,
The love He has for you.

To restore and strengthen, build you up,
Grow strong in perseverance.
Grow strong in love, grow strong in peace,
Let it wash away the tears.
Grow strong in grace, grow strong in healing,
Let Me wash away your fears.
For I see your heart, I see your mind,
I created you for a reason.
I knitted you in your mother's womb,
Created for a season.

The season of life, the season of love, the season of joy for Me,
The season of love is never ending,
The love I give to thee.
So take hold, take strength,
Take all you need to grasp.
Take My love and hold it tight,
My love is built to last.

It endures through darkness,
It endures through every situation.
It endures through the heaviest heart,
It gives you sanctification.
It gives you rest when you are weary,
It gives you peace when you are lost.
It gives you a stable foundation,
It is love that is never lost.

Be still and know that I am God.
Be still and feel My love.

Be still and take refreshment,
From the One who sits above.

I see your hurt, I see your pain,
I walk with you in the valley.
I do not stop, I never give up,
I am here for you.
I gave My son, a hefty price,
A ransom paid with love.
To wash you clean, to make you whole,
The greatest gift of love.

So arise, step out, I see your heart,
I know the thoughts inside.
Walk in My ways, follow My Word,
Keep pure your thoughts and eyes.
Do not let the enemy win, bring you down,
Fill your heart with lies.
Declare My love, declare My Word, it cannot
be undone.
Declare the love of Jesus,
The battle is already won.

Go out to those around you,
Declare My joy and peace.
Declare Jesus Christ the Saviour,
The blessings will not cease.
Declare the healing on your heart,
Declare love's purest form.
Declare the love of Jesus,
In Him your heart's reborn.

Declare the Father's love for you,
Declare the cleansing of your heart.
Declare you are victorious,
Declare you're Heaven's heart.
Declare you are victorious,
Declare you are strong,
Declare the victory of Jesus.
Declare Heaven's song.
Holy Holy is the Lord God almighty,
Who was and is to come.
Holy Holy is the Lord God almighty,
In Him is where I belong.

The Saviour's prayer is powerful,
The Saviour's prayer is strong.
The Saviour's prayer calls people home,
Home to where you belong.

God bless.

Blessed be the Name of the Lord

Job 1:20

"...Naked I came from my mother's womb,
And naked shall I return there.
The Lord gave, and the Lord has taken away;
Blessed be the name of the Lord."
In all this Job did not sin nor charge God with wrong.

Psalm 41:1-2

Blessed is he who considers the poor;
The Lord will deliver him in time of trouble.
The Lord will preserve him and keep him alive,
And he will be blessed on the earth;
You will not deliver him to the will of his enemies.

Your heart is pure, Your mind is true,
My grace and favour, rest upon you.
Although you cannot see the source,
I bring you this message, stay the course.
For I have a plan for you, that you cannot see,
Plans for good, plans to be.
The Leader, the driver, the maker, the key,
To bring home many, many to me.
To restore the lost, heal the sick,
To bring about change, to help those in need.

Your heart is pure, your mind is true,
I have not forgotten, nor forsaken you.
I walk with you in daily prayer,
I walk with you because I care.
I hear your heart, I hear your voice,
I come to strengthen you and your choice.
To reach out to Heaven and call it down,
The manner from above, the gifts around.
Call upon Me and I will provide,
Call out your needs from deep inside.
Call out to Me your deepest desires,
And watch My spirit work, the burning fires.

Flames to cleanse and to renew,
Flames that will lift and carry you.
My Holy Spirit is all around,
My Holy Spirit is always found.
Deep within the softest heart,
Always present, always ready.
He longs to be with you in every choice,
He longs to be your inner voice.
He longs to be with you in all your thoughts,
He longs to take part in your daily courts.
Of choices made and laughter found,
Of loving your family ever bound.
To you and your heart is where He belongs,
He will lift you up and keep you strong.

Don't despair and don't lose heart,
He is always present, right from the start.
He lifts you up to new horizons found,

He lifts you up to new blessings abound.
Blessings of which you cannot see,
Blessings received, ordained by Me.
Blessing your heart, blessing your mind,
Blessings of love you'll truly find.

For I know your heart is true and pure,
I know your family you truly adore.
I will provide much more than this,
Eternal peace, sealed with a kiss.
From your Heavenly Father who loves you so,
With joy I give to you below.
Favour, money, rich in love,
As gentle and loving as the dove.

I love you so deeply, I will not fail,
For I am the wind, blowing your sail.
To the land of riches here and now,
To bring you great joy, and peace much more.
Far greater than what you had before.
Joy unspeakable, joy so rich,
Joy of life and love abound.
Like the trees grow up from out of the ground.
I have planted in you many seeds,
From these acorns grow many trees.

So don't despair and don't feel down,
Lift up your heart and praise be found.
Inside your heart and outward call,
To your Father in Heaven who provides you all.
And receive My love, receive My grace,

Put out your tent pegs, widen the space.
To receive with love all I have to give,
To bring joy to you and watch you live.

A life restored, a life renewed,
For you have been faithful, you have been true.
To your word, to family, and to Me,
And so My mercies present you will see.
Grace and blessing, favour and love,
I supply to you and your family from above.
To give you a new life and new direction,
To build you up and make you strong,
Walk with My Holy Spirit, it's where
you belong.
Sing out loud and sing out to Me,
Together we will walk, you and Me.

Together in song, together in life,
Together we journey, you and your wife.
Together as a family, big and strong,
Together in spirit, secure and strong.
Together in love as one accord,
Together in peace, love adored.

"Be strong and do not lose heart for as it is written".

1 Corinthians 2:9

"Eye has not seen, nor ear heard, Nor have entered into the heart of man the things which God has prepared for those who love Him."

The Train Wreck

Psalm 57:9-10

"I will praise You, O Lord, among the peoples;
I will sing to You among the nations.
For Your mercy reaches into the heavens,
And Your truth unto the clouds."

Standing at the station,
Waiting for the train,
Waiting for the moment,
To end all this pain.
To step out into darkness,
One single step in fear,
For nothing can save me,
There is no one near.
No one who can help me,
To take away this pain,
No one who can love me,
For I have too much shame.
I have a past, I have a present,
That no one can know,
And so I must step forward,
And so I must go.
To whatever and wherever,
To take away the pain,
To leave this place forever,
Never to be again.

But stop and listen, listen to the voice,

The voice crying out from Heaven, the voice of Heaven's love.
I made you just the way you are,
I made you before all this.
I made you for so much more,
So much more than this.

For now is but a moment,
A moment that will pass.
Take My hand and walk with Me,
To the ever-last.
I know your heart, I know your past,
I see the things you've done.
I took all those things through my Son.
For Jesus paid the price to save the lost and the broken,
And now He stands right next to you.
So hear the words He has spoken.

I love you and I care for you.
So much more than you can know.
I care so deeply for you,
I cannot let you go.
I cannot let you step out now,
And end all of your life.
For who would take care of all your things, a baby, a child, a wife?

My love for you is greater, than anything you
are facing,
My love has overcome, the demons who
are chasing.
They have no power over you,
They have been defeated.
All you have to do is step back, no sin can
be repeated.

I took it all at the cross.
I took the sin and shame,
I took your pain and suffering,
To give you a fresh start.
Turn around and walk with Me,
Repent and start anew.
No eye has seen, nor ear heard,
What I have in store for you.
Of riches abound, beyond desire,
A heart restored, renewed.
Your new life is amazing, you have yet to see
My view.
Of what I have and where we will go,
Of wonders far and wide.
Of blessings falling from Heaven, with Me
standing by your side.

To help you on your journey,
No shame or condemnation,
A new heart, a new beginning,
Such was Jesus's demonstration.

The power of His suffering, upon the
wooden cross,
Will restore your life, remove your sorrows,
Take away the lows.
I will fill your heart with love again,
So you will love yourself.

I will fill your heart with love again to love
all mankind,
I will fill your heart with love again,
pure in love and grace.
I will fill your heart with love again,
put a smile on your face.

So step back and walk away, from danger oh
so present,
Walk with Me on a journey, I promise to
always stay.
Close by your side forever, and never
walk away.
Close by together, hand in hand,
an adventure through life.
An adventure through the mountains,
the mountains of life.
Of highs and lows and seasons,
of times for different things.
Times for glorious moments, when all the
angels sing,

Halleluiah, glory to the Father,
For He has overcome.
Halleluiah praise to God in Heaven,
The battle for you He won.
Halleluiah praise to God above, His love is glorious,
Halleluiah praise to Jesus, His work done on the cross.

Psalm 94:19

"In the multitude of my anxieties within me,
Your comforts delight my soul."

Psalm 94:22

But the Lord has been my defense,
And my God the rock of my refuge."

Psalm 95:1-7

Oh come, let us sing to the Lord!
Let us shout joyfully to the Rock of our salvation.
Let us come before His presence with thanksgiving;
Let us shout joyfully to Him with psalms.
For the Lord is the great God,
And the great King above all gods.
In His hand are the deep places of the earth;
The heights of the hills are His also.
The sea is His, for He made it;
And His hands formed the dry land.
Oh come, let us worship and bow down;

Let us kneel before the Lord our Maker.
For He is our God,
And we are the people of His pasture,
And sheep of His hand.

REDEMPTION

Deliverance from sin:

The promise of God to deliver us from the power and presence of sin. To be forgiven, holy, justified, free, adopted, reconciled to God through Christ.

Prophetic Artwork: The Power of Prayer through Jesus Christ

The image portrays the gospel of hope through a new life, new relationship and a new freedom in Jesus Christ. The viewer can see the many aspects of prayer: prayer for someone or a situation, prayer by someone, receipt of prayer, and the transformational power of Jesus Christ through all prayer. It is the gospel story in one image: the transformational power of the work on the cross to bring restoration to mankind and ultimately, where there was once death, there is now new resurrection life.

The foreground shows hands clasped in prayer at a table. The table is in reference to the scripture "You prepare a table before me in the presence of my enemies. You anoint my head with oil. My cup runs over" Psalm 23:5 (NKJV). It is a safe place to pray. It reminds the reader that our Father in Heaven is always available to us, regardless of the situation we may find ourselves in. There is always a time and place to pray, even if it does not look like the inside of a church. Our Father in heaven is always searching for people who need answers to prayer.

The rainbow bookmark within the pages reminds us how God is always for us and will never leave us, as He promised us through His creation of the rainbow. The lamp stand represents our place in a physical dimension: red, white and blue for our English heritage; green and gold for our current home in Australia. The rings on the lampstand represent the Heavenly realm: red for humanity/flesh, and blue for the Holy Spirit. The lamp stand is symbolic of the light of the gospel. It lights our path, providing security and clarity in otherwise dark and confusing situations.

The artwork leads the viewer to a person in deep thought and anguish, looking for guidance. The viewer may not know everything about the person or situation, but they can find peace knowing that God does.

Central to the artwork is the contrast of emotional anguish with joyous celebration. The person in red represents the fleshly body bound up, deep in thought and anguish. This person is sitting on their knees, emotionally, physically and spiritually burdened. The issues in their life are physically holding them down. The person on their knees is humble before God in prayer, desperate for guidance regarding a situation. This could be a person trapped in addiction, thus bondage in the form of chains, then breakthrough of a situation or relationship shown by the open padlock. Contrast this with the person in the blue, who represents the transformed soul or situation. The arms are stretched out wide in celebration of the victory received through the divine intervention of Jesus.

By His victory on the cross we have victory through Him in our lives. The watch on the wrist points upwards to heaven and is coloured red to represent the victory found in the blood of Jesus at the cross. Jesus is our true north and is symbolized by a red compass arrow.

The floor is coloured purple to highlight the Holy place where prayer is received in the throne room of heaven. Chains are shown to be literally broken, representing the freedom found in Jesus through the resurrection power of the cross. No longer slaves to sin, Jesus has broken us free from guilt and condemnation. The bread and wine depict the transformational power of communion, an act that aligns our hearts with heaven and brings heaven's reality to earth. It is a sacred time with God where we remember Jesus' sacrifice on the cross.

Jesus hears all our prayers; He is the key to all knowledge and understanding. He can unlock any situation or issue, no matter how bleak it may currently look.

Proverbs 3:5-6

Trust in the Lord with all your heart and lean not on your own understanding.

The sunflowers at the foot of the image represent the power of the gospel. Sunflowers face towards the sun as we should always look to God's son, Jesus, for our strength, guidance and nourishment.

In the foreground are hands symbolizing prayers spoken over someone or a situation. The person clasping their head with their hands should look to Heaven for guidance and truth rather than focusing on the stress surrounding the person or situation. As written in Colossians 3:2, "Set your mind on things above, not on things on the earth". Whether you are praying for someone or receiving prayer, continue on with life until you see or receive breakthrough and continue after the breakthrough with praise and thanksgiving.

1 Thessalonians 5:16-18.

Rejoice always, pray without ceasing, in everything give thanks, for this is the will of God in Christ Jesus for you.

The centre of the picture shows the breakthrough of God in that situation, transforming the person from being on their knees in duress to standing in victory and thanksgiving. This spiritual breakthrough is represented by the curtain/veil being torn as Jesus ascended to Heaven.

Matthew 27:51 (NKJV)

Then, behold, the veil of the temple was torn in two from top to bottom; and the earth quaked, and the rocks were split.

The earthly image is the person wearing the blue t-shirt with arms wide raised toward Heaven. It is a celebration position of posture acknowledging the freedom received through the power of Jesus Christ. He died and overcame death and sin for each of us. Through this act of love we begin to change on the inside and become more Christ-like. As we change our mindset and turn away from sin we are refreshed and cleansed through the power of the gospel.

Acts 3:19

Repent therefore and be converted, that your sins may be blotted out, so that times of refreshing may come from the presence of the Lord, and that He may send Jesus Christ, who was preached to you before.

He tore the veil so that all had access to Him anywhere and not just the priest of the church in the Holy place.

Isaiah 17:7 (NKJV)

In that day a man will look to his maker, And his eyes will have respect for the Holy One of Israel.

Job 19:25-27 (NKJV)

For I know that my Redeemer lives, and He shall stand at last on the earth And after my skin is destroyed, this I know, That in my flesh I shall see God Whom I shall see for myself, And my eyes shall behold, and not another. How my heart yearns within me!

Ask yourself the following questions:

What does deliverance mean to me?

Do I believe it? If not why not?

What does the bible say?

What actions can I take to change this mindset?

What action will I take to change this mindset?

Motherhood

A mother's love is never done,
A mother's love is never won.
It is a gift from God.

Matthew 18:1-5

At that time the disciples came to Jesus, saying, "Who then is greatest in the kingdom of heaven?"
Then Jesus called a little child to Him, set him in the midst of the, and said, "Assuredly, I say to you, unless you are converted and become as little children, you will by no means enter the kingdom of heaven. Therefore who-ever humbles himself as this little child is the greatest in the kingdom of heaven. Who-ever receives one little child like this in My name receives Me.

I see you in the morning,
I see you in the night.
I see you with your heart wide open,
I see you in the fight.
I see the hurt and passion, that overwhelms your soul,
I see the love inside your heart, to shelter them from the cold.
To give is such a beautiful thing,
A gift so rare and true.
A gift I placed deep in your heart,
A gift that represents you.

Do not worry or close it off,
For it is not your burden to bare.
Open wide, let the love flow,
Your heart was made to care.
For the hurt and needy,
For the lost and the sick.
For all who are in need,
Love pours out from you so quick.

I see the pain, I see the hurt,
Of what was meant to be.
Open up and release it,
Give it all to me.
I take the pain of a thousand souls,
I take the anger too.
For such an action I freely take,
Such deep love I have for you.

I care so deeply for your heart,
I care that you would feel so lost.
I care for the hearts of all My children,
That's why My son paid such a cost.
I know the feeling, to lose a son,
I know it cuts so deep.
I know the pain and suffering,
It runs oh so deep.
But once those feelings are released,
And handed over to Me.
Then your eyes can be opened,
Then you will truly see.
That all things happen for a reason,

And of all things I am in control.
All things work together for good,
To win back so many souls.

I do not expect all things to make sense,
Or to show you all the reasons.
I come to bring you the gift of love,
The gift that endures all seasons.
A gift so rare and precious,
A gift I give to you.
A gift you openly give to others,
That gift defines you.

For you open up your heart,
And freely give to others.
You are love personified,
A standard to all mothers.
So cry out loud and cry now,
Release the pain you feel.
Cry out and rejoice with Me,
Divinely your heart healed.
Cry out in love, cry out in joy,
Cry out to the heavens above.
Cry out with all you have inside,
Restore your heart of love.

You bring about peace to everyone,
Just like the lilly-white dove.
I love you deeply _____,
So deeply beyond words.
So deeply I watch over you,

Like the shepherd of the herds.
You care for all your children,
With passion and with praise.
You lift up, you take care of them,
Forever till the end of days.
A mother's gift is inside you,
And witnessed for all to see.
So sing out, stand tall, head up,
Come, walk with Me.
For there are times to withdraw,
There are times to be sad.
There are times when our heart aches,
We do not feel glad.
But love is the greatest gift,
That gift I gave to you.
That gift of life flows outwards,
It is what you do.

So love all and love me,
You know that I love you.
I love you in the valleys,
I love you on the hills.
I love you in the mornings,
I love you in the night,
I love you everlasting,
I love your heart and soul.
I love you ever present,
I love you more than gold.
I love you more than rubies, or any other stone.
I love you for being faithful,
I love you for being you.

I love you, I love you, I love you,
I love you, I truly do.

Psalm 139:17

How precious also are your thoughts to me, O God!
How great is the sum of them!
If I should count them, they would be more in number than the sand;
When I awake, I am still with you.

God's Provision

Matthew 6:26-34

Look at the birds of the air, for they neither sow nor reap nor gather into barns; yet your heavenly Father feeds them. Are you not of more value than they? Which of you by worrying can add one cubit to his stature? So why do you worry about clothing? Consider the lilies of the field, how they grow; they neither toil nor spin; and yet I say to you that even Solomon in all his glory was not amazed like one of these. Now if God so clothes the grass of the field, which today is, and tomorrow is thrown into the oven, will He not much more clothe you, O you of little faith? Therefore do not worry, saying, "What shall we eat?" or "What shall we drink?" or "What shall we wear?" For after all these things the Gentiles seek. For your Heavenly Father knows that you need all these things. But seek first the kingdom of God and His righteousness, and all these things shall be added to you. Therefore do not worry about tomorrow, for tomorrow will worry about its own things. Sufficient for the day is its own trouble.

In the quiet of the day,
I have much to say, of plans I have for you.
In the quiet of the day,
I have much to say, I wish to talk with you.

I wish to show you visions,
Of life's riches far and wide.
I wish to show you where to place your feet.

I wish to show you how to walk,
In your destiny far and wide.
If you would rise with Me and not hide,
I wish to show you who to meet,
I wish to show you who to greet,
It's not a chore for Me.

For I will feed you more each day,
If only you would rise and pray.
I wish to speak with you more.

I am a God of promise, I am a God of truth,
Of love abound and more.
I am a God who loves you,
I am a God who cares for you.
I am truth, the light, the way.
So rise up early in the mornings,
I have a lot to say.

Of riches I have a store full,
Heaven is where they live.
So call down on My promises,
I will truly give.
To those who speak out My blessings,
So rich and far they reach,
To those who hear My Word,
For those whom I love to teach.

I care for you so deeply,
I care for you so much.

Open My bible, declare My promises, seek Me
and I will touch,
All areas of your life.
All your hopes and dreams,
All issues of the heart.
Healed, restored are broken dreams.
For out of your heart flow the issues of life,
So rich and so powerful are they.

Open up your bible and read with Me,
I have a lot to say.
I want to teach you mercy,
To forgive and forget.
I want to teach you restoration.
Of standards I have set.
My Son forgave so many,
Even though he died upon the cross.
He forgave the worst of mankind.
For they were truly lost.
He forgave the ones who loved Him.
Even though they showed no will.
He forgave the soldier with the spear,
The very one who killed.

And so you must forgive your brothers,
Don't harbor such a grudge.
For if you don't forgive others,
You too will be judged.
I know your heart pains deeply,
For all the hearts mistrust.
But give your anger unto Me,

And I will set you free.
Give Me the pain deep down inside
I want to take it away.
Give Me the hurt and deception
Today is a new day.

A day of hope, a day of love,
Of promises rich and new.
A day of shedding old thoughts,
Today is a new you.
Today is for renewed life,
Of promises, rich in love.
Today is a new beginning,
Sent from your Father above.
Today I want to restore your heart,
It beats with love and honour.
Today your life is changing,
Reach out to your brother.

For who knows the thoughts inside a heart,
Except your Father in Heaven.
Who knows the power of redemption,
A divine gift from heaven.
Let go, release your paintings,
And open up the love.
And I will pour out My blessings to you,
Blessings sent down from above.

Do not worry, do not be scared,
For I know what you need.
Do not worry about the harvest,

For first you must plant the seed.

The seed of love is powerful,
It grows beyond our dreams,
It grows in the darkest places,
It grows beyond our dreams.
To places we cannot see.
Places far and wide
Places of restoration, places in the mind,
Places where we love each other.

There is no greater gift.
Places of family and communion,
Watch as your spirit lifts.
To joy and celebration,
A family restored
To Heavenly saturation,
A true gift from the Lord.

For Jesus paid a high price,
To give you a clean heart.
He paid the ultimate sacrifice.
For mankind a new start.
So go out and open up,
Declare your love for Me.
Declare the restoration, and see what will be.

Plans of love and hope renewed,
I watch over you each day.
My plans I will show you,
If you would only pray.

So rise up and find your quiet place,
And listen to My voice.
To forgive and forget, and move on,
I will mend your heart.
To forgive and forget, a truly divine new start.

Be strong and courageous,
I will walk with you.
Be strong and courageous,
I love you, I truly do.
I love you in my love,
I cover you in grace,
I cover you in blessing
Shine bright with Heaven's glory.
Put a smile on your face.

I care for you so deeply,
In me place your trust.
For Jesus died upon the cross,
He paid the ultimate cost.
To bring love and restoration,
To redeem the lost and broken.
Breathe in these words I have given you,
They are Heaven spoken.

To build you up and restore you.
To help you understand.
That love is the greatest gift
To be given to every man.
Do not hold back or withdraw
For from Me love is truly given.

For My son died on the cross,
But now He is risen.

So go out from this moment,
And let things that have happened be.
And I will show you love profound,
Love given to you from Me.

Romans 8:28

And we know that all things work together for good to those who love God, to those who are called according to His purpose.

Spirit of Adoption

Esther 5:14

"For if you remain completely silent at this time, relief and deliverance will arise from the Jews from another place, but you and your father's house will perish. Yet who knows whether you have come to the kingdom for such a time as this?"

Esther 8:6

"For how can I endure to see the evil that will come to my people? Or how can I endure to see the destruction of my countrymen?"

Ecclesiastes 3:1

To everything there is a season.
A time for every purpose under heaven:

John 4:13-14

Jesus said to her, "Everyone who drinks of this water will thirst again, but who-ever drinks of the water that I shall give him will never thirst. But the water that I shall give him will become in him a fountain of water springing up into everlasting life."

Proverbs 5:18

"Let your fountain be blessed,
And rejoice with the wife of your youth."

The joy that is in your heart,
It is a special gift.
Pour out your love on others,
In them it will surely lift.
Lift up their hearts, open their eyes,
To what the world can be.
Lift up their hearts, open their mouths,
Of what I did for thee.

I came to bring them love.
I came to bring them peace.
My love outpoured through your body,
The river of love will not cease.
I come through you with giftings,
Of which you have many.
I come through giftings unseen.

For all things come in seasons,
A time to sow seeds.
A time to reap the harvest.
A time to nurture children.
A time to see them grow.
A time of love and understanding,
In you I placed such gifts.
For you are a guardian of children,
So powerful and rich.
You care so much and nurture so well,
I am proud to call you Mine.
For you cultivate the minds of children,
A gift so rich, so divine.
I do not give this often,

For such is a time as this.
For caring for the children,
It is the greatest gift of gifts.
I see the love you outpour,
I see the blessings given.
To preach the message to children,
My child, how He has risen.

To save a world so lost,
To save a world so cold.
To implant this message of truth,
Before their hearts are old.
You have a responsibility,
Of which you live it well.
My good and faithful servant,
Whom else could I tell.

Of hopes and dreams of many,
Of generations to come.
Words spoken over children,
Words spoken by a mum.
The mother of a generation,
The mother in whom I trust.
The gift of speaking over them,
No matter what the cost.

I give you all My blessings,
Poured out of Heaven above.
I give you all My resources,
For you do truly love.
To nurture and to protect,

The motherless generation.
To go and witness far and wide,
The far off forgotten nations.

Do not be scared, do not be fearful,
For I have broken all their chains.
Do not be scared, do not be subdued,
For My son Jesus reigns.
Over all situations,
Over all circumstance
Over all issues of the heart,
For you will truly dance.

A dance of celebration,
A dance of joy and peace.
For out of your heart flows the river of life,
Of love and of peace.
I know you are fearful of what this will all be,
But trust me when I tell you,
I will walk with you, “Come, follow Me”.
I will take you to far-away lands,
To heal the lost and broken.
I will take you to far-away cities,
To speak the words Jesus has spoken.

I will lift you up,
I will give you knowledge.
I will help you speak out loud,
To heal all the children.
Reach up to the Heavens,
And cry out for My Word.

I will give you the anointing,
To speak across the land.

I will stand beside you,
Strengthen you with love.
I will stand in battle,
Your Father from above.
I will hold you as we walk,
I will give you the words to say.
I will speak into your heart.
In visions, one each day.

For though your gifting is visual,
And you wonder how it comes,
Your visions travel through the land,
Like the beating of the drums.
They travel far and wide,
Further than you think.
They travel right through barriers,
Through eyes to think,
Of God's beauty present, visual and true,
This gift of drawing My love,
This gift I have given you.

So reach out to My children,
And send out the message far and wide.
Step out and release My love,
From this you must not hide.
For I have planted within you,
A gift so pure and true.
A gift I rarely give out,

A gift I give to you.

So from this place we walk together,
My hand is holding yours.
My eyes will give you visions,
Your hands will be renewed.
To paint the love I show you,
To paint the world I see,
For Jesus died upon the cross,
He died for you and me.

To bless the world My children,
To overcome the hate.
To restore and sanctify souls,
To rid this earth of hate.
To build up and restore love,
For there is truly no better gift.
So open up your easel,
And watch their spirits lift.

Rise up and take your place,
For there is such a time as this.
Rise up and cover the world's heart,
With the love of a mother's kiss.

Luke 2:51

The He went down with them and came to Nazareth, and was subject to them, but His mother kept all these things in her heart. And Jesus increased in wisdom and stature, and in favor with God and men.

The Orchid in the Vase

An orchid is to be placed inside a vase. The gentle, brittle nature of the orchid is protected in the best vase available. As the vase is valuable, you need strong hands to hold the vase and solid ground so that you do not trip over and drop it.
The orchid is protected in the vase whilst it has been taken from the vine. As the water in the vase is renewed and tended, the orchid remains strong and beautiful until it returns to the earth. The more it is tended and refreshed the longer it will last. Its beauty comes from the vine but is sustained by the water and the tending hand. Should the vase, the vase carrier, the water or the tending hand become less than God intended, it will show in the diminished beauty of the orchid. Each must be strong and stable, nurturing and refreshing in order to display God's full beauty.

Song of Solomon 2:10

My beloved spoke and said to me;
"Rise up, my love, my fair one,
And come far away.
For lo, the winter is past,
The rain is over and gone.
The flowers appear on the earth;
The time of singing has come,

And the voice of the turtledove
Is heard in our land.
The fig tree puts forth her green figs,
And the vines with the tender grapes
Give a good smell.
Rise up, my love, my fair one,
And come away!"

Proverbs 18:22

He who finds a wife finds a good thing.
And obtains favor from the Lord.

Proverbs 31:31

Give her of the fruit of her hands,
And let her own works praise her in the gates.

Beauty is a spiritual thing,
Beauty is heard when you sing.
Beauty is a way of life,
Beauty is within a wife.
For though you stand in crowded rooms,
You do not feel the strength to bloom.
But I stand with you, I stand strong,
To help you release your heart of song.
Released to all for Heaven's glory.
Released to all, sing My story.

Of Christ's love for all mankind,
Christ's love everlasting.

Christ's strength, love renewed,
Christ's peace, pain subdued.
Sing out My love and open your heart,
Sing to the heavens where it will start.
To reign down blessings from mercy's seat,
Reign down My love upon your feet.

And as you walk across the floor,
My love will fill you more and more.
To reach the lost and the broken,
To sing to multitudes the words I have spoken.
Words I will give you, inside your heart,
Words to change nations torn apart.
Words are powerful, words are strong,
Words change lives, through My song.

I will speak to you, deep within,
For your heart is pure, removed of sin.
A pure connection God ordained,
The Holy Spirit, He will remain.
To bring you the strength, to sing out loud,
To stand at the front and lead the crowd.
For I created you to sing My song,
At the front is where you belong.

I gave you a strength you have not seen,
I gave you a belief, to be a queen.
To represent My kingdom, here on earth,
For such is My love, such is your worth.

I care for you more than you know,
I will not forsake you, this you know.
For the day will come, when you will see,
Just how precious you are to Me.
A voice of love, a heart of truth,
A standard of beauty, to reach the youth.
To sing with angels, Heaven aloud,
To sing My glory, a wonderous sound.

Redemption, resurrection, love so pure,
All the world I do adore.

In a crowded room

Psalm 94:19

In the multitude of my anxieties within me,
Your comforts delight my soul.

Sitting in a crowded room
Wondering what to say.
Can I think of something neat
To help you end your day.

Do I know the thoughts you think?
Will they be good enough?
Can I relate to your intellect?
Do you think this way?

I feel the love of the Father,
You comfort my isolation.
You speak when I hear silence,
You calm all my frustration.

The noise of silence is deafening.
In a room so full of men.
I cannot think of what to say
In such a masculine den.

Help me to relate to these
Godly men of old.
Help me to communicate
Bring warmth to my cold.

I feel your love, I speak your words
But in a crowd I feel silent.
This ache inside to speak out loud,
Inner turmoil, violent.

Be still and know that I am God,
I called you for a reason.
So speak the words I have given you,
For now is a new season.

No more looking back at things,
No more isolation.
No more deathly silence heard,
No more inner frustration.

You think the words are for Me
But how many feel this way?
How many without the cars and the sport,
Have nothing else to say.

So though they speak out so many things
They do not bare their souls.
Help them to look deep inside
Feel My warmth in the cold.

We are here to love and help
The lost in isolation.
We are here to speak to all
The Saviour, our true salvation.

So speak to them about My love
About My Holy Spirit.
Help them to understand My love
Help them to truly live it.

For though the noise is deafening
I hear silent hearts.
Though the noise sounds like happiness
I hear saddened loss.

Though you sit in silence
Your presence speaks out in volumes.
Though you sit in isolation
I surround you in love adored.

Enjoy the fellowship of My love
Enjoy the friendships formed.
And when the thunder rages in,
Stand together in the storm.

For man was never meant to be alone.
Not even in the beginning.
For helpers, lovers, friends unite.
This will stop man sinning.

For where love is, love must grow,
Where seeds are planted, fruit must grow.
Where souls stand united in love,
A three-cord strand cannot be broken.

Pick up My Word and speak it out.
The day has just begun.
Speak My words to all walks of life.
Christ died and now is risen.
Risen to set the captives free.
Risen to speak to you and Me.
Risen to lift the heavy heart.
Risen to give a transformed start
Risen to love the lost now found.
Risen in love, in love now bound.

Risen to love humanity.
Risen for you, risen for me.

The love of the Father reaches into the hearts of men and transforms the hardest of hearts, the broken and the sick. There is no soul he cannot reach.
Come to Me, come quick.
Salvation is open to one and all.

Proverbs 8:17

I love those who love me,
And those who seek me diligently will find me.

Acts 10:34-35

Then Peter opened his mouth and said: "In truth I perceive that God shows no partiality. But in every nation whoever fears Him and works righteousness is accepted by Him.

1 JOHN 4:10

Beloved let us love one another, for love is of God; and everyone who loves is born of God and knows God. He who does not love does not know God, for God is love. In this the love of God was manifested toward us, that God has sent his only begotten Son into the world, that we might live through Him. In this love, not that we loved God, but that He loved us and sent His Son to be the propitiation for our sins. Beloved, If God so loved us, we also ought to love one another.

2 PETER 3:9

The Lord is not slack concerning his promise, as some count slackness, but is longsuffering toward us, not willing that any should perish but that all should come to repentance.

Two are better than one

Ecclesiastes 4:9

Two are better than one,
Because they have a good reward for their labour.
For it they fall, one will lift up his companion.
But woe to him who is alone when he falls,
For he has no one to help him up.
Again if two lie down together, they will keep warm;
But how can one be warm alone?
Though one may be overpowered by another,
two can withstand him.
And a threefold cord is not quickly broken.

Many roads you have travelled
Many places you have seen
Many hearts have been healed
Many tears in between.
Though some have stayed and some moved on,
Your wife is beside you, and the love of
My Son.

I have seen your hurt,
I have seen your pain.
I have walked alongside you, through the wind
and the rain.
Through the storms of life you have sheltered
the needy,
With My lavish gifts you have not been greedy.

Passed into you and through you,
I have blessed many.
Never taking your own, not even a penny.
My faithful son, in whom I am pleased,
I will adorn you with gifts,
As you pray on your knees.

My Spirit washes you and cleanses your heart.
Over the years you feel it has been torn apart.
By people and humanity, for such is the need.
I need master craftsmen, to sow the new seed.

Of love and forgiveness,
as the end times draw near
To spread out My love, drive away fear.
I will show you new sights, visions and dreams,
Glorious new beginnings, majestical themes.

For you have run your race and passed on
the baton.
Now is the season to look to the future.
Nurture and guiding, living and loving,
For mankind is growing and mankind is dying.
My love endures endlessly through the
enemies lying.
I call to your heart, would you trust me
once more?

As I show you a new path,
As I show you a new door.

Walking together, husband and wife
Walking together in a new season of life.

I know the scars you both have on your hearts,
I know the fears when given a new start.
I know the blessings that come from obedience
I know the joys you long for, in the world
of experience.

I care for you deeply, trust this you must know,
So I bless you and guide you, before you go.
I will show you new insights, new visions
of life.
I will grow your hearts closer, husband
and wife.

I will repair and restore your desires within.
I will refresh your mindsets, cleanse you within.
For now is the season, a time of great blessing.
Now is the season, for you to start confessing.
My Word to many about the grace I have given.
Now is the season of how Christ is risen.

For you know My love, you know
my restoration.
You give from your heart, without hesitation.
But now I wish to bless you both,
Now I wish to show you more
Now I wish to open the door.

To new and lavish gifts, physical and heavenly.
Wondrous visions, your heart cannot see
Beautiful journeys, walked with Me.

I will take you both to places far and wide
I will protect you and your family,
I am right by their side.
The reward of the faithful is not to be missed.
The love I wash over you, richer than a
first kiss.
It renews and restores, all history washed,
Energised, cleansed, removed life's cost.
For I bathe you in My love,
Let me restore your heart.
To give and to love, going back to the start.

Fresh grace, fresh anointing, new
chapters begin,
I will restore your strength, deep within.
I will restore your courage, faith even more,
Like a palace guard, stood at the door.
Protecting all who reside within.
Protector of family love deep within.

I will resource your army,
For battles ahead.
I will furnish the grain house.
There will be bread.
So much to give, to the people who come,
So much joy from the songs that are sung.
So much love from My Spirit given freely

To those in need, the broken, the weary.
I will bring about blessings and promises of old,
I will provide food and shelter to those out in the cold
l will restore the lost and the broken
l will complete the words I have spoken.

I will bring you new leaders, helpers and friends
A well that is feeding, its source never ends
To help you achieve your visions of old
To help you achieve new visions so bold
That will show you My capacity to renew and restart.
The yearnings you feel, deep within your heart.

So go out in love, excited to see
The blessings and outpourings I have for thee.
For your faithful service has always been seen.
Life's treasures in your hands, you have gleaned.
The smiles of life, the laughter of joy.
The excitement of love, between a girl and a boy.
The Father's love is washing you clean,
Ready for a journey yet unseen.
But be still and know that I Am God,
Your Father in Heaven, looking down from above.
Take My hand and walk with Me together
My love surrounds you, together, forever.
In love and in life, beauty restored,

A husband and wife, both adored.
Rest and enjoy your travels together
My love for you both will last forever.

Isaiah 54: 2

Enlarge the place of your tent,
And let them stretch out the curtains of your dwellings;
Do not spare,
Lengthen your cords,
And strengthen your stakes.
For you shall expand to the right and to the left,
And your descendants will inherit the nations,
And make the desolate cities inhabited.

Matthew 25: 23

His Lord said to him, "Well done, good and faithful servant;
You have been faithful over a few things,
I will make you a ruler over many things.
Enter into the joy of your Lord.

The Father's Love

1 John 2:29

If you know that He is righteous, you know that everyone who practices righteousness is born of Him.

1 John 4:12-16

No one has seen God at any time. If we love one another, God abides in us, and His love has been perfected in us. By this we know that we abide in Him, and He in us, because He has given us of His Spirit. And we have seen and testify that the Father has sent the son as Savior of the world. Whoever confesses that Jesus is the son of God, God abides in him, and he in God. And we have known and believed the love that God has for us. God is love, and he who abides in love abides in God, and God in him.

Through the fields we walk and talk
Of cities old and new.
Many steps we have travelled together
My voice, I have given you.
To speak of old things born again,
To set the captives free.
To open up the closed hearts of many,
My righteousness through thee.

I've walked with you through fields of fire,
I've shown you pastures green.
I've taken you to faraway places

Some you've never seen.
But now I take you on a journey
Of depth and love most true.
This depth of heart I work inside,
I work inside of you.

For though you see my spirit visions
You do not always look.
To see the words I have for you,
My words inside your book.
For it is a book for all mankind,
It is a book for you.
It is a conversation, we talk,
But now I talk about you.

You have had such a hard few months
Of this there is no doubt.
But all the time your heart is steadfast,
My words you do still shout.
To heal the sick, find the lost,
To set the captives free.
But now I speak to matters close,
Matters close to thee.

The challenges though they are real,
Are overcome in prayer.
And this you know each day you walk
So speak the prayers to share.
For many have heard my words through you
And many have been saved.

And so many will lift your prayer
With arms to heaven raised.

I feel your love, I feel your pain,
I know your deepest fears.
I know your intimate thoughts and feelings,
Conversations spanning years.
I have not ever let you down
I do not intend to start
For when I called you to Me
I knew you were set apart.

Set apart brings challenges,
Of this you know all too well.
But look back at the victories
Of these stories, many I hear you tell.
So speak of these victories, past, present, future
And dream big adventures, you and your wife.
For vision creates reality
And reality is your life.

For love abounds within you both,
And love will always stay
Close together in unity,
For you two that is the way.
So fear not what stares at you,
Be still and know I am.
Be still and speak to your mountain
For within you, you know I can.

Lean on my Spirit inside of you,
And hear my lion roar.
And open up the heavenly realm
Calling healing through your door.
For mighty is My man of God,
And know that man is you.
Speak My words over your situation
This is what I called you to do.

You speak it over others,
You do not hesitate.
Speak My words over your situation
Daily meditate.
And watch the situation change,
And see My work in you.
And know that this personal mountain
Is just another mountain to you.

You speak into everyone else,
And now I speak into you.
I love you, you are My son
And I am proud of you.

I called you on a journey
Which has a narrow path.
But now we get to have some fun,
Now we get to laugh.
I will take you places
You never could imagine.
You will know it's Me.

For I will show you many things.
Things others cannot see.

So take this time to enjoy,
The love I bring to you.
And see My work in your life
And what I will do for you.
For you know My promises are Yes and Amen,
For those who know My name.
And we have walked together for so long
We have played the game.

So now I call to you once more
Hear the words I say.
"I love you dearly, I trust you more,
A fresh word given each day.
Know that I love you,
Deep inside your heart.
Know that I love your wife
I love her very heart.

I see you both, I love you two
A couple so in love.
I bless you both in the heavenlies,
Love sent down from above.
I love you both, I love you now
I love you ever more.
I love you here and eternity
Hear my angels war.

For they stand guard around you
To walk in all you do.
And they do not stop fighting
This promise I give to you.
So sing out and sing up,
To heaven high above.
And feel My presence pour down on you
From Heaven high above.

I know your heart, I know your pain,
I know you know My Word.
But let these words envelop you
The loving balm of My Word.
To cover you into love's great joy,
To cover you in peace.
My love poured out over you
In abundance it will not cease.

So sing out loud and sing out clear,
Raise your hands to Me.
My glory and My majesty
In your life, for all to see.

I love you in the moment,
I love you all the time.
I love you in all seasons.
Know that you are Mine.

Love poured out abundantly
from a cup that will never run dry.
For Jesus Christ our Lord and Savior

Our King seated up high.
Seated next to the Father
Seated next to you.
Seated in the heavenlies.
Ever present, watching you.

1 John 3:16-23

By this we know love, because He laid down His life for us. And we also ought to lay down our lives for the brethren. But whoever has this world's goods, and sees his brother in need, and shuts up his heart from him, how does the love of God abide in him? My little children, let us not love in word or in tongue, but in deed and in truth, and shall assure our hearts before Him. For if our heart condemns us, God is greater than our heart, and knows all things. Beloved, if our heart does not condemn us, we have confidence toward God. And whatever we ask we receive from Him, because we keep His commandments and do those things
that are pleasing in His sight. And this is His commandment: that we should believe on the name of His son Jesus Christ and love one another, as He gave us commandment

Matthew 6:25

Therefore I say to you, do not worry about your life, what you will eat or what you will drink; nor about your body, what you will put on. Is not life more than food and the body more than clothing? Look at the birds of the air, for they neither sow nor reap nor gather into barns; yet your heavenly Father feeds them. Are you not of more value than they? Which of you by worrying can add one cubit to his statue?

MATHEW 8:13

Then Jesus said to the centurion. "Go your way; and as you have believed, so let it be done for you." And his servant was healed that same hour.

Hope

Ester 5:14

For if you remain completely silent at this time, relief and deliverance will arise from the Jews from another place but you and your father's house will perish. Yet who knows whether you have come to the kingdom for such a time as this?

Hebrews 13:2

Do not forget to entertain strangers, for by so doing some have unwittingly entertained angels.

The man in the can is part of My plan,
He feeds from the trash of life.
The man in the can has a powerful story,
A family and a wife.
We look upon the homeless,
We frown or fall apart.
Seldom do we stop to think,
about a person's heart.

But if you stop to think, you stop to pray,
You wish you had the words to say,
"Come. Sit down, let's talk.
I would love to hear your story.
I would love to hear of your walk.
I would love to speak of Jesus,
Of all He has done for me.

I would love to show you His love
And what He wants to say to thee.

He cares about your family,
He cares deeply about you.
He cares about your childhood,
He cares about your life.
He cares so much He wants to speak of things
that appear lost.

Yet He has found you here today,
He sent an angel to you.
To help you and to feed you,
He sent a beautiful lady,
Who has showed you His love.
He wants to have a relationship,
He wants to walk in your life.
He wants to re-establish love, a husband and
a wife.
Will you let Me in, to talk with you?
And show you how much I care.
Will you let My angel in?
She only lives over there."

You have a heart so open,
It is a pleasure for Me to watch.
Your love abounds so mercifully,
I will bless you and your ways,
I will show you visions, places and
journeys past.

I will show you new adventures, memories
to last.
A lifetime of adventure, the list is long
and known.
But now I come to show you
Thy harvest, from the seeds you have sown.

Seeds that were scattered,
Seeds that you thought were lost.
Seeds I watched you plant.
I saw just what they cost.
But now is the time to get ready
For many blessings will follow.
Now is the time My love pours out
To end your season's sorrows.
For I have seen the end, the start and
the beginning
And I have chosen such a time as this
For you to dance and be singing.

Of joyous celebrations, of love and
laughter too.
Of the children born of the Spirit, but children
birthed from you.
I know the feelings you have, feelings so dark
and scared
But remember these words you are reading
Remember the words you've heard.
For I am a God of promise, and promises
I keep.
There was a time of sorrow

But now is the time to reap.
Now is the time to celebrate
Now is the time to sing.
Of praise like you have never heard.
Of songs of joy and love
Songs from choirs of angels
Songs from your God above.

I am the God of truth, I am the God of love,
I am the God of blessings, promised
from above.
So call them down from Heaven,
Call them down to you.
Call them down in wondrous songs
My prophet I give you the view.
Of lands abound with plenty
Lands abound in love
Lands abound in beauty
Crowned with wondrous love.
I am the God of majesty,
Of blessings that you have seen.

Remember the promises I gave you,
Remember what we have seen.
Remember the words I spoke to you
So young, so rich and fair.
Remember the promises you have written
For I gave you them with care.
To nourish and to water
To gently watch them grow.

To give you fruit in plenty,
Seeds for new ones to sow.

Seeds that will start a new fire
Fire deep down in your heart.
Seeds that will start a new life,
A generation to start.
So bring in the harvest and welcome,
The souls of new beginnings.
Bring in the adventures,
In Heaven angels are singing.

A chorus rich in love abounds
A chorus strong and true.
A chorus rich in Heaven's love
A love to cover you.
Be strong and be obedient
In all that comes your way.
For this is the greatest testimony, you will
ever say.
Of how I keep My promises
Of how I keep My word.
Of how I keep the faithful,
So close within My herd.

I give you these words of wisdom
To keep your faith so strong
I give you these words of love
The words of Heaven's song.
For you have been so faithful
You have stood the test of time.

And now the world will know this
Now the world knows you are Mine.

I leave you peace, I leave you love,
I leave you in this joyous season
I leave you these words to read over,
For now you have a reason
To celebrate and wash away
The thoughts of darkness past.
For now these thoughts are heavenly
A love that is built to last.
For I am love, I am truth, I am the light ahead.
And I am the God of promises, and that is what you have read.
Take peace and love, My gifts to you
And celebrate in spirit.
Hold on to My seeds of happiness
You are truly going to live it.

2 Corinthians 1:20

For all the promises of God in Him are Yes, and in Him Amen, to the glory of God through us.

The Watchers

Daniel 4:1

Nebuchadnezzar the king,
To all peoples, nations, and languages that dwell in all the earth;
Peace be multiplied to you.
I thought it good to declare the signs and wonders that the Most High God has worked for me.
How great are His signs,
And how mighty His wonders!
His kingdom is an everlasting kingdom,
And His dominion is from generation to generation.

Daniel 5:14

I have heard of you, that the Spirit of God is in you, and that light and understanding and excellent wisdom are found in you.

The watcher's heart is a heart of peace,
The watcher's heart does not cease.
Visions plain, visions true,
Holy forecasts I give to you.
For I see more than you can see,
But this gift of vision I give to thee.
To see the mountain, to see the valleys,
A word in each season, to encourage.

Lift up your head, open your eyes,
The Spirit speaks, oh so wise.
Of love and healing, of joy and sorrow,
For who knows what comes, out of tomorrow.
I love you deeply and watch over you,
And place this gift in your heart,
For others to view.
Of mercy, love, intercession,
The joy and peace from Christ's resurrection.

I give you My sight for all to see,
The closeness of love, My walk with thee.
To lands afar, rich in love,
To intercede in nations,
Guided from above.
I give you peace and honour too,
For this is My gift, I give to see.
Speak My heart, speak My words,
Speak the joy of Jesus Christ.

For all will know I speak to them,
Through the words I give to you.
For all will know the love I have,
For you will be on, in view
To address the nations of battle,
To speak of love and peace,
The Father's love for His children
A love that never will cease.

Be strong and be courageous,
For some will not believe.

Be strong and be courageous,
For some will want to leave.
For not all hear My words,
Their hearts are hardened to it.
Their eyes are closed with envy, lustful
unclean thoughts.
Of battles they want the victory, brought
through the courts.
But My court is the open land,
The land on which I built.
And I will have My prophecy,
And now you will see them tilt.
For nothing is stable and nothing is secure,
Except the love of Jesus.
Now and forever more.
He came and paid the price of love,
He died for all our sins.
He died upon a wooden cross,
For hearts, he died to win.
And nothing happens on this earth
That is not the Father's will.
His love for humanity
No earthly action can kill
For He is love, He is truth, the way, the light,
the I Am.
He washes over everything, He does because
He can.
So write down all your visions
Keep them plain and keep them known
For mysteries of a time to come
To you they will be known.

I give you My love, I give you My sight
To help all those in need
To end the pain and suffering
To end the lust and greed.
To end the perversion of mankind
And bring them back to Me
To open their eyes to My love,
The love I have for thee
So speak out your heart and the words I give
They will not return void
For from the Father's belly I give you words
to speak,
My words will not return void.
My words will cut through hearts,
My words will lift and encourage.
For I am the God of fresh starts,
I am the God of glory,
Of victory and praise.
I am the God of Heaven,
I will teach you My ways.

I will teach you how to love,
How to speak to hearts.
I will give you eyes to see,
To see each new fresh start.

For I can see in your heart,
The heart you have for Me.
And I can trust you to speak My words,
Words that impact lives.
Words that impact families,

Words that impact wives.
Words to build up Godly men,
Of valour and of truth.
Words of light and wisdom,
Restore their lost, misspent youth.

Words to grow their wisdom,
Words to reach their hearts.
Words to bring back lost dreams,
Words that mean fresh starts.
Words that impact lives,
Words of truth and love.
Words from your heavenly Father,
Sent down from Heaven above.

Words to break open deserts,
To let My love flow in.
Words to cleanse, redemption,
Words to wash away sin.

Words of knowledge, words of truth,
Words of God in Heaven.
Words are life to your bones,
To your soul.
Words are My sword in Spirit.
My words are the truth, the way,
I only ask you to live it.

So speak up and speak out,
Give them what I have to say.
And walk the harvest to come in,

Watch it start today.
Watch it open Heaven's heart,
To all whom I draw in.
Watch Me break open closed hearts,
Wash away their sin.

Watch Me open their eyes,
To see the love I am.
Watch Me open their ears,
The sound of love I am.
God blesses you and your family,
For all your walks of faith.
He cares deeply for all of you,
He helps you on your way.
Blessings will be outpoured,
From Heaven unto the earth.
For nothing is too big for the Father,
For in Him you are blessed.

So go out to the nation,
Give them what you see.
Give them My words and encouragement,
And I will protect thee.
I will keep you safe from harm,
Protected and adored.
For many illnesses you have overcome,
A testimony of love,
Of how the Father loves His children,
And watches from above.

Psalm 33:13-15

The lord looks from heaven,
He sees all the sons of men.
From the place of His dwelling He looks,
On all the inhabitants of the earth;
He fashions their hearts individually;
He considers all their works.

Psalm 33: 18-19

Behold, the eye of the Lord is on those who fear Him.
On those who hope in His mercy,
To deliver their soul from death,
And to keep them alive in famine.

Psalm 33:20-22

Our souls wait for the Lord.
He is our help and our shield.
For our heart shall rejoice in Him,
Because we have trusted in His holy name.
Let your mercy, O Lord, be upon us,
Just as we hope in you.

Psalm 14:2

The Lord looks down from heaven upon the children of me,
To see if there are any who understand, who seek God.

The Seeds of Your Heart

Psalm 62:5-8

My soul, wait silently for God alone.
For my expectation is from Him.
He only is my rock and my salvation;
He is my defense,
I shall not be moved.
In God is my salvation and my glory;
The rock of my strength,
And my refuge, is in God.
Trust Him at all times you people;
Pour out your heart before Him;
God is a refuge for us.

Philipians 4:6-7

Be anxious for nothing, but in everything by prayer and supplication, with thanksgiving, let your requests be made known to God; and the peace of God, which surpasses all understanding, will guard your hearts and minds through Christ Jesus.

Proverbs 4:20-23

My Son, give attention to My words;
Incline your ear to my sayings.
Do not let them depart from your eyes.
Keep them in the midst of your heart.
For they are life to those who find them.
And health to all their flesh.

Keep your heart with all diligence.
For out of it spring the issues of life.

Seeds are placed in your heart for it is the most
fertile ground.
Seeds are placed deep within,
To shelter it from the sound.
The sound of fear and discouragement,
They reach in to steal your peace.
But I placed them deep, like a mustard seed,
To allow them time to grow.
To strengthen and to take root,
To develop and to sustain.
To make deep roots, way down deep,
Through adversity they will remain.

So keep them fed and watered,
For this I gave you My Word.
It has the power to bring to life,
All that you have heard.
All that you have spoken,
All that you have seen.
All that I have given you,
And now, the unseen.
So speak to Me from inside your heart
Help Me to cleanse it free.
Free of all negativity,
Free to establish Me.

All My hopes and dreams for you,
I placed them deep within.

All covered over and protected,
Wiped clean of all your sin.
For My Son came to cleanse you,
To redeem and sanctify.
To free the lost and broken,
To give them a new start.
And from the fertile soil they grow,
The issues of the heart.

So do not be down, do not be sad,
I have given you many a seed.
Read and study, proclaim My Word,
And live out My dream.
That mankind will learn to love each other,
With gentle love and care.
That mankind would learn to love again,
And reclaim the love of their Heir.
To riches from within the kingdom,
Rich so bound in love.
Riches to be released to My children,
Riches deep in love.

So guard your hearts and nurture,
For the soil is rich and true.
Guard your heart with My love,
The eternal love I have for you.
Pray and speak My Word over it,
And watch the seeds, they grow.
And reap the fruit of the harvest,
The good fruit that you sowed.
Rejoice and praise your Father,

Be glad in all that you do.
For many will watch your actions,
And watch me walk with you.

Believe and have strong faith,
It will carry you through the valleys.
Believe and have strong faith,
It is the strength of our marriage.
Of relationships and love bonds,
That cannot be broken.
Given strength and encouragement,
By My words that you have spoken.

Words to build and words to live,
Words to declare My Sovereignty to you.
Words of everlasting joy, eternal love,
Words of power and meaning.
Words of declaration, to reach up to
Heaven's ceiling.
To bring down to earth the kingdom,
The blessings of love and joy.
The blessings brought through relationship,
Between a girl and a boy.

A union together,
A union born to love.
A union sanctified in Heaven,
A union blessed from above.

So go out into the kingdom,
Declare these words of truth.

Declare them to all mankind,
Especially the youth.
For they are in need of encouragement,
Of strength and salvation.
Of a Father's love that covers them.
A Father's love, so true.
A Father's love eternal,
Eternal just for you.

Ephesians 1: 17-21

"that the God of our Lord Jesus Christ, the Father of glory, may give to you the spirit of wisdom and revelation in the knowledge of Him, the eyes of your understanding being enlightened: that you may know what is the hope of His calling, what are the riches of the glory of His inheritance in the saints, and what is the exceeding greatness of His power toward us who believe, according to the working of His mighty power which He worked in Christ when He raised Him from the dead and seated Him at His right hand in the heavenly places, far above all principality and power and might and dominion, and every name that is named, not only in this age but also in that which is to come."

Change Your Perspective

Change Your Perspective
From perplexity to peace
From confusion to contentment
From fearful to faithful

Habakkuk 3:18-19

Yet I will rejoice in the Lord,
I will joy in the God of my salvation.
The Lord God is my strength;
He will make my feet like the deer's feet,
And He will make me walk on my high hills.

I walk with you on the mountaintops
I walk with you in the valleys.
I walk with you in the season of life,
I walk with you in love.

I see your troubles, I see your foes,
I bless your hands to work.
I hold you tightly, I hold you close,
I will not let you go.

For on this journey many will see
The love I pour out on thee.
Many will look upon this story
Many will call to Me.

For I will listen, I will call, the people home
to Me.
Through the love of My Son, Jesus Christ,
I will restore their lands.
Through the blood of the Lamb, Christ, ever
last,
I will renew their hands.

To work in union, restore and renew,
A Christ-centred life.
As your marriage is restored
As your heart has grown
As your love is towards your wife.

These words I give to bring you hope,
To show you how much l care.
To lift you up when the crowds surround.
And the people begin to stare.

For I mark this day as the beginning and end.
A day of renewed blessing.

For My love to pour out to the ill and broken.
I give you the anointing to preach the
unspoken.
Words of love and connection.
To declare what is not.
To break the bonds
Through the power of Christ's resurrection.

For He died that you live,
He hurt that you healed,
He cried that you may rejoice.

A mantle is given, for Christ is risen,
To be carried from Father to Son.
And on this day, I will hear you say
The battle is already won.

So step out in Faith,
Declare Christ's love.
Call down provision from your Father above.

Walk in Faith.
Build in love.
Declare Christ's Love
And glory to God in Heaven above.

Be strong and true, just be you.
And I will do what I said I would do.
For it is a Yes, it is an Amen.
I will complete the work I have given.
You cannot "hide" in the light.
Write down the words I give to You.

John 12:46

"I have come as a light into the world, that whoever believes in me should not abide in darkness".

John 1:5

"And the light shines in the darkness, and the darkness did not comprehend it".

2 Corinthians 3:6

"For it is the God who commanded light to shine out of darkness, who has shone in our hearts to give the light of the knowledge of the glory of God in the face of Jesus Christ".

Matthew 5:16

"Let your light so shine before me, that they may see your good works and glorify your Father in heaven".

Psalm 119: 105

"Your word is a lamp to my feet And a light to my path".

Your Word

Your Word is an ointment to my bones.
It soothes my innermost being.
It restores my hope.
It guides my feet
It renews my heart.
It renews my mind
It breathes into my soul.
It corrects
It restores, It heals
It loves
It nurtures
It is love.
It is peace
It is truth
It is a very present help
It is an ever present help.
It is life itself.
It is the Word of God.

Because it is all the above, why would you not speak it over yourself, your family, your friends, your work, your future, your situation, your recommended "Everyday seeds of life".

I am changed

Psalm 94:19

In the multitude of my anxieties within me,
Your comforts delight my soul.

I've been changed.

Psalm 23:4

Yeah, though I walk through the valley of the shadow of death, I will hear no evil.

I've been changed.

Psalm 22:22

In the midst of the assembly I will praise You,

I've been changed.

Psalm 3:14

You, O Lord, I lift up my soul.
O my God, I trust in You.
In You, O Lord, I put my trust;
Let me never be ashamed;
Deliver me in Your righteousness
Your mercy is unending

PSALM35:9

But as for me, I trust in You, O Lord,
I say, "You are my God."
And my soul shall be joyful in the Lord,
It shall rejoice in His salvation."

I walk through this fire, though my flesh
burns alive.
I feel no pain in the spirit for my
heart is being refined.
I rejoice at the trial I encounter,
It brings me closer to Your love.
There is no greater Father, than our Father,
Abba, above.

You rush in and lift me up,
Your arms are strong and true.
Though my body is weak,
Your Love is not,
That is why You are You.

I Feel Your love, I know You are near,
If I only opened my ears, I would hear,
The sound of angels crying out,
"Hallowed be Your name."

Christ is here, he is Lord,
Victory has been before us.
Though I cry out to You, I feel regret,
The presence of my sin.

I listen to Your spirit call,
He uplifts me from within.

I feel His peace, I feel His love
There is no truer friend
He knows my name, he knows my soul
His love will never end.
Rejoice and bathe within My love
You are so precious to Me.
Rejoice and bathe within My love
Open your heart and see.

That all life's trials and all life's hardships
They too soon will pass.
And out from within emerges,
A strength and love ever last.

I feel Your love,
I feel Your grace
I feel the gaze of my Father's face.

A gaze of love,
A gentle smile.
This righteous reveal,
Let it stay a while.
And comfort my soul, deep within
Remove the ache from the deepest sin.

For redemption came at such a cost,
For all our lives. His was lost,
For all our shame, He was shamed,

For all our hurt, He was pierced
For all our addictions, He was inflicted
An exchange of love, His Word predicted.

This Word is yours, use it well,
For grace is given, for you to tell.
Of resurrection, battles won
Through the exchange of the Father's son.
He endured so that you would declare,
The price of victory, your soul aware.
It beats in time with Heaven's drum,
It beats in tune to the Father's son.

Hold fast and true, divine love renewed
My peace I give you,
Conviction of love renewed.
My soul is tender, my heart fragile,
In Your presence, I will stay awhile.
To fill my soul with the Saviour's love
l rejoice in the manner I receive,
The Fathers love.

For it sustains me, in my desert place
It gives me strength until I see His face.
Then all at once, my heart is healed.
The love of the Father has been revealed.

There is no pit He cannot reach,
No circumstance He cannot teach.
Of Christ's love, and restoration,

He is with you in an instant,
No hesitation.

Be still and know that I Am God,
Be still and know that I am within.
Be still and know that I see your trials,
Be still and know that I forgave your sin.

For I sent My Son, to redeem and restore,
I sent My Son to end the war,
The perfect sacrifice to atone for man
Dating back to when the earth began.

My promises are true, they do not change
Yet man cannot comprehend, to him
it's strange.
That a Father's love would endure
Throughout the ages, more and more.
Yet here we are and I am true.
Just like My love, My love for you.

I do not lie, I only love
As a Father should, reigning down from above.
I love you My child
This you must know.
For there is nothing you can do to make
Me go.

I am here in the valleys,
I am here in the joys.
I am here victorious for all girls and boys.

For this is how I see you
Through a Father's eyes
None of My children will I despise.

For love is the greatest, a gift so true,
Love is My gift, My gift to you.
So stand up and praise, raise your
love to Heaven
Restore you I will, what the locusts ate,
times seven.
Restored, renewed, victorious in love,
My child you are seated next to My Son
in Heaven above.

So wipe your tears and rejoice with Me.
For you do not yet see, what I see.
A child of God, dressed in righteousness
Through My Son Jesus you are righteous.
Blemish free and pure and true.
This is My gift I give to you.

Restored, renewed, loved and cherished,
It is My joy to remove such a blemish.
For My love is great. My gift of restoration,
My gift to you without hesitation.

2 Corinthians 5:17

Therefore, if <u>anyone</u> is in Christ, he is a new creation; old things have passed away; behold, <u>all things</u> have become new.

Romans 8:37-39

Yet in all these things we are more than conquerors through Him who loved us. For I am persuaded that neither death nor life, nor angels nor principalities nor powers, nor things present nor things to come, nor height nor depth, nor any other created thing, shall be able to separate us from the love of God which is in Christ Jesus our Lord.

Love

MATTHEW 22:37-40

Jesus said to him," You shall love the Lord your God with all your heart, with all your soul, and with all your mind." This is the first and great commandment. And the second is like it; "You shall love your neighbour as yourself." On these two commandments hang all the Law and the Prophets.

MASK 12:29

Jesus answered him," The first of all the commandments is." Hear, O Israel, the Lord our God, the Lord is one. And you shall love the Lord your God with all your heart, with all your soul, with all your mind, and with all your strength. This is the first commandment. And the second, like it, is this:" You shall love your neighbour as yourself." There is no other commandment greater than these."

Love is a balm to my soul
It nurses the deepest wounds.
It covers the darkest of sins
It rejoices from the open tomb.

Love is the call on mankind
A gift so rich and rare
Love is the saviour of many
It is how we are taught to care.

Love breaks the chains of bondage
Love speaks into the heart of man
Love endures the winter storms
Love is as the earth began.

It cries out to the lost and broken.
It heals the sick and lame
It strengthens the married union
In the spirit, in the flesh we proclaim.

Love can move mountains,
Love abides within,
Love is a healer, redemption,
Love is where we begin.

Speak the songs of love to all,
Speak My love to the many
Show My love in your daily walk
Giving to all and needy.
For out of love grows all things
A never-ending supply
But cut it off and look ahead
The relationship will die.

For love prunes, love renews,
Love holds a thousand hearts,
Love restores, love is patient,
Protector from the enemy's darts.

Steadfast and true, a gift to you.
Hold it tight and don't let go.

A song of joy, a song of peace
A presence you will feel.

Take My love, feel it within,
Let the Spirits' restoration begin.
A thousand heartbeats, a thousand embraces.
Love restored on nation's faces.

People rejoicing, people singing,
Love creates a new beginning.
Where hearts are open, minds are too
Let the love flow, the Spirit renew.

And all will see the great reveal,
The love I gave to beak the seal.
To show mankind what I hold dear
To speak the words you long to hear.

I love you so much I sent My Son.
He loved you so much. He made sure it was
done.
Death on the cross, dead and hidden
Three days later, gloriously risen
An act of love for all to see
An act of love, a call to thee.

A love so strong it cannot be broken,
A love united, souls called when spoken.
Bondages broken, chains removed
Hearts' desires, cleansed, renewed.

Walk in love and you will see
It is the greatest gift, a gift to thee.
Embrace the love, a Father's heart,
Then you will see revival start.

When the body loves and the body moves,
Bitterness, jealously will all be removed
And songs will be sung, scripture spoken
Delivered souls, re-awaken, to all the
Love the Father has.
A love so deep, it never runs dry,
Eternal peace that will never die.
Live in love, walk in faith
Confess your sins and be renewed.
Receive My Love, My joy.
Restore, renew your hearts.

1 Corinthians 13:1-13

Though I speak... And now abide faith, hope, love, these three; but the greatest of there is love.

You are chosen

John 15:15

No longer do I call you servants, for a servant does not know what his master is doing; but I have called you friends, for all things that I heard from My Father I have made known to you. You did not choose me, but I chose you and appointed you that you should go and bear fruit, and that your fruit should remain, that whatever you ask the Father in My name He may give you. These things I command you, that you love one another.

Isaiah 45:1-8

"Thus says the Lord to His anointed,
To Cyrus, whose right hand I have held.-
To subdue nations before him
And loose the armour of kings,
To open before him the double doors,
so that the gates will not be shut:
"I will go before you
And make the crooked places straight;
I will break in pieces the gates of bronze
And cut the bars of iron.
I will give you the treasures of darkness
And hidden riches of secret places,
That you may know that I, the Lord,
Who call you by your name,
Am the God of Israel.

For Jacob My servant's sake,
And Israel My elect.
I have even called you by your name;
I have named you, though you have not known me.
I am the Lord, and there is no other;
There is no God besides me.
I will gird you, though you have not known me.
That they may know from the rising of the sun to its setting.
That there is none besides Me.
I am the Lord, and there is no other.
I form the light and create darkness.
I make peace and create calamity,
I, the Lord, do all these things.
"Rain down, you heavens from above,
And let the skies pour down righteousness,
Let the earth open, let them bring forth salvation,
And let righteousness spring up together,
l, the Lord, have created it.

Deuteronomy 7: 6-8-9

For you are a holy people to the Lord your God: the Lord your God has chosen you to be a people for Himself, a special treasure above all the peoples on the face of the earth.
The Lord did not set His love on you nor choose you because you were more in number than any other people, for you were the least of all peoples, but because the Lord loves you. and because He would keep the oath which He swore to your fathers, the Lord has brought you out with a mighty hand, and redeemed

you from the house of bondage, from the land of Pharoah king of Egypt.
Therefore know that the Lord your God, He is God, the faithful God who keeps covenant and mercy for a thousand generations with those who love Him and keep His commandments

Understand your destiny to understand your calling. Understand your responsibility to future generations and descendants.

Look to heaven and you will see
I have a place set aside for thee
A place to be seated at the right hand side of My Son,
A place I chose, you did not win.
For first I must remove your earthly sin.

An exchange of love, renewed, redeemed,
A precious stone, once dirty now cleaned.
Shining highly for all to see
Shining bright through My love to thee.
Bought at a price you could not pay
Eternal grace, the righteous way
Traded at the cross, pain endured
Your Father's gift, a heavenly reward.

So walk in love, let not your brothers fall,
Heed My calling, Speak My words to all
A voice in the darkness, to bring light,
A voice of righteousness, that won the fight.

To save mankind and walk in love
A Father's heat, poured out from above.

I will guide you, keep you safe.
I will teach you what to say,
I will sustain you in seasons' tides,
I will never leave you, My love abides.
Worship and praise are your battle armour
Scripture and discernment your sword of truth
Armour of God to protect our youth.

Raise them strong, raise them in love
Raise them to show their Father's love.
Raise them into all they can be
A life of compassion, a life in Me.
I will lead you in all your works
I will teach you My intimate thoughts.
I will protect you and fill you with grace
Seek refuge and strength in our secret place.
For I have called you to speak to the nations
I have called you out from temptations
I have removed the thorn in your side
Removed they will stay, if in me you abide.

Don't look back, only look ahead
For looking over your shoulder will cause
yon dread.
Know that I am, and I have you covered
Know that I love you for you are My beloved.
Know that I Am, and always will be,
Know that I love you, you are precious to Me.

Bought at a price no one else could pay
Bought out of love, renewed this day
Bought for a purpose, a destiny called
Bought out of sin, My love endured.
Help those in need.
Do all that you can
Follow My guidance, stick to the plan.
For many will come, and many will read,
The words that I gave you,
Those words will become seed.

For many lives will be touched
And many will be saved
You cannot fathom the extent of the
pathways laid.
Of thousands of souls all marching
home.
Millions of people rejoicing in love
Generation after generations, saved by My love.

For I will not stop calling people to Me
There is no corner to hide, not under the sea.
For I know where My children are
And I know what they need.
And so they will benefit from the crop of
My seed.

Sow in this season and endure for a while
You soon will see My love and your smile.
Of riches stored up in Heaven's house above
Riches called down from Heaven above.

Riches to furnish My kingdom on earth
Rather to sustain the future of church.
Riches to support my children's worth.

Souls and people, invested in.
The love of My Son, removed their sin.
The love of My Son will renew and rebuild
The love of My Son calls out in the field.
To reap the harvest of works done before
To fill up the barns, replenish the stores.
To teach and to show My majesty.
My grace and favour in a world so torn
How My son loves mankind,
How mankind can be reborn.
Through the gift of love
Bought and paid in full
Born again in Christ, love forgives.
For after death, three days risen.

To love and lead, to renew the earth.
To bring souls to heaven, eternal worth.
Rise up and sing, Rise up and praise
The Father's love will shine through these days
And give hope to mankind
And love to the needy.
Restore what was lost and take from
the greedy.

For love will endure, love will renew
Speak these words I give to you.
Lift up the lost.

Love those who fall
Take up My cross
Step into your call.
For you were chosen
I paid the price
I called you on purpose
No roll of the dice.
I set you apart for a specific task
Follow my calling
Into eternity, everlast.

JEREMIAH 1:5

Before I formed you in the womb I knew you;
Before you were born I sanctified you:
I ordained you a prophet to the nations.

JEREMIAH 1:9

Then the Lord put forth His hand and touched
my mouth, and the Lord said to me:
"Behold I have put My words in your mouth.
see, I have this day set you over the nations and over the kingdoms,
To root out and to pull down,
To destroy and to throw down.
To build and to plant.

JEREMIAH 1:17

"Therefore prepare yourself and arise,
And speak to them all that I command

you."

The morning after a spiritual attack, where I was pinned to the ceiling. my spirit is at peace thinking towards heaven rather than what happened in my sleep.

Confidence

Isaiah 55: 10-11

That it may give seed to the sower
And bread to the eater,
So shall my word be that goes forth from my mouth;
It shall not return to me void,
But it shall prosper in the thing for which I sent it.

Isaiah 54:4

"Do not fear, for you will not be ashamed;
Neither be disgraced for you will not be put to shame;
For you will forget the shame of your youth,
And will not remember the reproach of your widowhood anymore."

Though you walk through the fields of life
You do not believe what you see.
Though you hear the words to speak to people
You wonder if they come from Me.

Do I speak them now, do I wait a while,
Do I tell my friends, do I say,
Do I preach the words you give to me,
Do I wait for another day?

But time waits for no one
And no-one waits for time.

So speak the words I give you,
For the truth spoken is Mine.

I will give you the words to speak out loud,
I will give you the knowledge to discern.
I will give you the verse to speak out.
Come with Me, on a journey to learn.

Learn how to speak in love,
Learn how to see and feel.
Learn how to discern good from bad
Learn what is truly real.

For I give you My knowledge, I gave you
My Spirit,
I give you the anointing to call,
I give you the voice of My righteousness,
To speak out to one and all.

As the sunshine breaks the skyline,
As the storms begin to clear.
So will My words come out from you
Let the captives begin to hear.

Of righteousness, and love abound,
The love of the Father in Christ we are found.
Saved by the blood of Jesus Christ
Redeemed, reborn, renewed.

Speak the truth in love and life,
Speak the words of eternity.

Speak the truth, the way, the light,
Of beauty found in Me.

Battleground, battle found,
Victory at the cross.
Put on your armour, speak My words
You will never be at a loss.
Weild the sword of the Spirit,
Speak My words of truth,
Let these words soak in your spirit
As the eagle renews its youth.

I will strengthen you, I will sustain you,
There is no place to hide.
Speak out My words of encouragement,
Speak them far and wide.

For beauty is in the eye of the beholder
And I see all that was.
I see all that is to be,
And I know what it cost.
For I gave up a precious gift,
To give mankind a start.
I gave you My only begotten Son,
To renew your hardened hearts.

So let Me in and let Me speak,
I will take you far and wide.
Learn to trust Me, learn to listen,
There is no need to hide.

For I will be with you,
I will teach you, just how to hear.
I will make you a warrior of Christ,
You do not need to fear.

Open up, let me in,
I will not force My way
Speak to Me, let us talk,
For we both have much to say.

I love you My child, I love you so,
I want the best for you.
Study My Word, let the scriptures absorb into
your body and soul.
For I want to build you up again,
I want to make you whole.
Washed in the blood of Jesus Christ, baptized,
in the spirit renewed.
I have begun a work in you.
Your mindset and spirit a renewed.

Free from sin, full of love,
Watched overhead from the Father above.
Made in My image, a daughter of Christ,
Paid in full, no roll of the dice.
Formed in the womb, known in Heaven,
Lifted up, fully forgiven.

Speak My words, live life in me,
Watch the miraculous unfold around thee.
Strengthened within, full of grace,

A born-again smile upon your face.
Cherished and loved, beauty so rare,
Eyes opened wide, now so aware.
To serve the lost, help the needy,
Broken hearts, repaired in victory.

I will walk with you, and you with Me
What marvelous wonders I have for thee.
Blessings stood up in heaven waiting,
To be called down to earth as gifts of love.
Presents from your Father above.

So speak the words I give to you.
You will be blessed in all you do.
Abundant blessings in all your days.
Sing to the heavens, a song of praise.

Let the words sing out loud,
Remove the skies of the dark clouds,
Glorious skies, open hearts,
Renewed hopes, life's fresh starts,
Seeds sown, harvests to come
Your renewed life has just begun.

Gracious and loved you are My child
Blessed and victorious in all you do.
Such is My love,
My love for you.

Psalm 46: 10

Be still and know that I Am God.

Hebrews 13:6

So we may boldly say:
"The Lord is my helper; I will not fear.
What can man do to me?"

Hebrews 10:35-39

Therefore do not cast away your confidence, which has great reward. For you have need of endurance, so that after you have done the will of God, you may receive the promise:
"For yet a little while,
And He who is coming will come and will not tarry.
Now the just shall live by faith;
But if anyone draws back.
My soul has no pleasure in him."
But we are not of those who draw back to perdition, but of those who believe to the saving of the soul.

Psalm 139:13-16

For you formed my inward parts:
You covered me in my mother's womb.
I will praise you, for I am fearfully and wonderfully made;
Marvelous are Your woks,
And that my soul knows very well.
My frame was not hidden from You when I was made in secret,
And skillfully wrought in the lowest parts of the earth.

Your eyes saw my substance, being yet unformed.
And in Your book they all were written,
the days fashioned for me,
when as yet there were none of them.

Justice

Psalm 40:8

I delight to do Your will, O my God,
And your law is within my heart.

Ecclesiastes 4:9-12

Two are better than one,
Because they have a good reward for their labor.
For if they fall, one will lift up his companion.
But woe to him who is alone when he falls,
For he has no one to help him up.
Again, if two lie down together, they will keep warm;
But how can one be warm alone?
Though one may be overpowered by another, two can withstand him.
And a threefold cord is not quickly broken.

Running the race of your life,
Amongst the strain and the strife.
Be encouraged by the love that surrounds you,
The love and care of your wife.

For out of these trials come blessings,
The fruits of your labour, yet unseen.
But seen in the heavenly realms they are,
Called down to you in joy.
The joy of the love a Father has,
The joy of a girl and boy.

Wrapped up and entwined in deepest love,
A love so deep and rare.
A love I blessed before you were born,
A love beyond compare.

Honour your love for each other
Your relationship is on the stage.
Honour your love in the quiet times
It will go on to a future age.

Your love warms the hearts of many,
Enduring, caring and free.
Your love for each other magnifies,
The love I have for thee.

Be blessed with these words of encouragement
For I wish to lift up your hearts.
Be filled with My love to each of you,
Each day is a new start.

So run your race in glory.
Under the grace of My Son.
Run your race in victory
For the battle is already won.

I love you both as My children
I love you both as parents.
I love you more each day you live
I love you more each season.

For My love is unending,
My love covers all sin
My love encourages all unions,
For this is where family begins.

So walk in love and celebrate,
Your family and blessings.
Celebrate the house of love
You've created for your family.

Celebrate My love poured out,
Celebrate My peace.
Celebrate My joyous life
Given to you through the cross.

Celebrate My love,
It endures, even in the loss.
Celebrate My victory,
For My Son died at the cross.

But though He died, many shall live
Redeemed, restored renewed.
Many will come to honour you,
For you have been renewed.

Washed in His blood, awakened,
Refreshed within your heart.
Ready for a new season,
Ready for a new start.

So gather your family and celebrate
The race is almost won.
Gather together your loved ones
Your new journey has begun.

A journey so rich in love and honour
So joyous beyond compare
A journey so deep in love for each other.
People can but stare.

For the love you have for each other.
Shines out like a burning star.
Your love for each other,
Is a testimony to others afar.

Be still and know that I am God
Take a moment to enjoy.
The love I gave to both of you.
The love between girl and boy.

Enjoy this new found season
A season rich in blessings
Speak love to, and over, each other
For there is much joy in the confessing.

The power of My Word will lift your hearts up
to and into heaven.
My words will unite your love in more ways
than you have seen.
My words will strengthen you,
On a journey where you haven't been.

To places rich in love and joy
Places of beauty and renewing.
Places where your hearts are entwined
In love and public viewing.

For I have blessed you all your days
I have called this time.
I have called you together,
The world will know you're Mine.

Forged in love and worship
Together for a lifetime.

Together through the trials of life
A love so pure and true
Together woven in spirit.
As My love is for you.

Proverb 5:18-19

May your fountain be blessed,
and may you rejoice in the wife of your youth.
A loving doe, a graceful deer
-may her breasts satisfy you always,
may you ever be intoxicated with her love.

Matthew 19: 4-6

"Haven't you read." he replied, "that at the beginning the creator made them male and female, and said, 'For this reason

a man will leave his father and mother and be united to his wife and the two will become one flesh?'
So they are no longer two, but one flesh. Therefore what God has joined together, let no one separate."

Ephesians 4:2-3

Be completely humble and gentle; Be patient, bearing with one another in love. Make every effort to keep the unity of the spirit through the lord of peace!'

Jeremiah 29:11

For I know the plans I have for you," Declares the Lord" plans to prosper you and not to harm you, plans to give you hope and a future"

1 John 4:7-8

Beloved, let us love one another, for love is of God; and everyone who loves is born of God and knows God. He who does not love does not know God, for God is love.

Love

Galatians 5:22

But the fruit of the spirit is love, joy, peace, patience, kindness, goodness, faithfulness.

Psalm 28:7

The Lord is my strength and my shield: in him my heart trusts, and I am helped; my heart exults, and with my song I give thanks to him.

Speaking into your heart.
My love is never far apart.
I see all that you do
Hearts opened and renewed.
Welcomed like a son
Loved like a daughter
Sacrificed a lifetime
The Lamb brought to slaughter.

An exchange of love and peace
My blessings will not cease.
For out of My heart flows
The love and grace of the kingdom
I know your heart's desires,
I hear your prayer requests,
Petitioned in love and honour
These are the prayers I blessed.

For out of the servant's heart
Flows blessings of milk and honey
Out of Heaven's cries
An attuned ear like a mummy.
The pain is heard,
The cries of love
Gentle touch
Just like the dove.

Peace reigns over all My children
Confessions made
Souls forgiven
Joyous moments of eternity
Gifts of love passed down from Me
Gifts of joy, I give to thee.

Prayer in all things, large and small,
Prayer builds people up, standing tall.
Prayer is union, Heaven called,
Prayer is sanctified, honoured blessed.
Prayer is righteous, stood the test.
So that all may know that I am God,
All may know the love of the Father
All may know I am here.
All may know My love reigns.

Keep praying, don't stop
Chains have been broken.
Lives saved from the words you have spoken.
Bondages removed, souls restored,
All from your lifts at the Father's accord.

For I search the land to act on prayer
And when I do, I see you there,
Calling down Heaven's angels to fight
Calling down the Father to fix what is right.

What is true and just I will not let go
In your heart, this you know.
So call on Me and together we will win
Together we will overcome
This world of sin.
Together in victory for the battle is won
Together in righteousness, the power of My son.
For Jesus died upon the cross for you
Saved and restored, My gift to you.

A gift so rich you understand
And now confess to others across this land.
That they may know the love of the Father
They may know My unending love.
They may call on Heaven above
They would see the love I am.
They would praise and serve the Lamb.
For worthy is the Lamb that was slain
For His name is all that will remain.

When judgement comes and I am He
Then mankind will finally see.
That My words do not return void
My words establish what I set out to complete
Save mankind on every street.
Save mankind in the fields and meadows

In the hills and mountain tops
In the remote parts of the hidden lands
Deserts, oasis, golden sands.
There is no place I will not reach,
Nowhere to hide, only teach.

My love will cleanse the souls of man
My love given freely, the saviour's plan
So call to those in your prayers
Call on Heaven to repair
Call on the Father seated on high
Call out My Word for it does not lie.

Call on Jesus to fulfill
The Spirit's guidance, the Father's will.
Call on the angels to receive all the
blessings of the Father's will.
Prayer answered. Faith active, never still
Speak up, speak out, act in love
Showed in grace, the Father's love.
Poured out from Heaven by your Father above.

Philipians 4:6

Be anxious for nothing, but in everything by prayer and supplication, with thanksgiving, let your requests be made known to God; and the peace of God, which surpasses all understanding, will guard your hearts and minds through Jesus Christ.

EPHESIANS 6: 14

Stand therefore, having girded your waist with truth, having put on the breastplate of righteousness, and having shod your feet with the preparation of the gospel of peace;
above all, taking the shield of faith with which you will be able to quench all the fiery darts of the wicked one. And take the helmet of salvation, and the sword of the spirit, which is the word of God; praying always with all prayer and supplication in the spirit, being watchful to this end with all perseverance and supplication for all the saints.

1 CORINTHIANS 14:1-2

Pursue love, and desire spiritual gifts, but especially that you may prophesy. For he who speaks in tongues does not speak to men but to God, for no one understands him; however, in the spirit he speaks mysteries.

The Love of the Father

2 Samuel 7:3

Then Nathan said to the king," Go do all that is in your heart, for the Lord is with you.

Jeremiah 29:11

For I know the thoughts that I think toward you, says the Lord, thoughts of peace and not of evil, to give you a future and a hope.

Jeremiah 29:12

Then you will call upon me and go and pray to me, and I will listen to you. And you will seek me and find me, when you search for me with all your heart. I will be found by you says the Lord, and I will bring you back from your captivity; I will gather gather you from all the nations and from all the places where I have driven you, says the Lord, and I will bring you to the place from which I cause you to be carried away captive.

I search the kingdom for fertile ground
Listening for My words to make a sound.
The sound of creation,
The sound of love
The Father's called from heaven above.
Seeds of joy, seeds of victory
Seeds of love to you in time.

Seeds are planted, seeds are watered
For the harvest in due time.

For I wish to bless My children daily
I wish to bless My people so.
I wish to cover them in love so dearly
Ever present, I won't let go.
For in My Word I declared love
Sent down as a Saviour from heaven above.
To bring love and restoration to all mankind
Freed from bondages that would have
you bound.

Unable to think, and dream and live,
Choking your creation like soil through a sieve.
But Jesus came that you may be free,
Sanctified, restored, washed clean by Me.
So take My hand, let us walk a while,
I will carry you down the aisle.
As a bride of Christ, loved and cherished,
Restored as new, you will not perish.
For I have many dreams I placed in you,
And you have dreams to accomplish too.

To take My hand and let us talk,
Together, side by side we must walk.
Sharing the love between a Father and daughter,
Sharing the love between a Father and son.
Sharing the love of Jesus Christ
Heaven's love that cannot be won.
For this love is given free of charge

Unending love poured out to you.
Take it, let it fill your soul
Let it soothe your weary heart.
Let it rekindle your imagination,
Let it drive inside a new start.

Of hopes and dreams and life's joys,
Fulfilling journeys fruit for toys.
Saved souls in a world of decay,
Captives freed from what you say.

So speak life, speak My truth,
From the babies to adults, the seniors,
the youth.
For all have come to hear My Word
All have come so let it be heard
That Jesus died on the cross for them
Three days later rose again.
Salvation calls you from despair,
Salvation begins once you declare.

Jesus as your Lord and Saviour
Jesus will come and change your behavior
A miraculous change from inside,
Nurturing love, pulling down pride.
Building you up in time and seasons
Heaven's called you for this reason.

To call out to the masses and speak My truth
Oh how the Father loves, from child to youth.
From teenager to adult, old age and more

For you I cherish, love and adore.
There is no pain I cannot heal
Pull you out from your ordeal
Love you, honour you, make you well
Redemption, redeemed, restored to tell.
I am love, I am truth, I am righteous,
ever caring,
Come to the Father, let Me heal your wounds,
Let us journey out together, out from
these tombs.

Free from death and captivity
Free from darkness, loneliness and despair.

Out into the light, you will find love there.
Love from your Heavenly Father, that's Me.
Joyous care and protection I give to thee.
To restore and renew your life's desires,
Fan the flames of heaven's fires.
To guide home all who find themselves lost,
None shall perish, My Son paid the cost.

Died on the cross to save mankind.
Died on the cross to open eyes of the blind.
Rose again in victory
Rose again for you to come to Me.

Take My hand let us walk.
Take My hand together we talk.
Open your heart, let Me help you inside
Take away anger, jealousy, pride.

These are a few of the human conditions
All destroyed by love when Christ had risen

So take your place, take My hand
Let us start today
All it takes is John 3:16 to say.
Jesus Christ is my Lord and Savior
Help me change, be like You in behavior
Pour out Your love upon me today
These are the words my heart has longed to say.

I need you Jesus, would you walk with me.
Open my eyes, and let them see.
The truth, the light, the way of heaven
You died on the cross, but for me You
have risen.
Take my life and make it Yours
Help me to be more like You each day.
Teach me to declare, teach me to pray.
Show me how to change my ways.
From this day forward, I declare my life
is Yours.

John 3:16

For God so loved the world that he gave his only begotten son, that whoever believes in him should not perish but have everlasting life. For God did not send His Son into the world to condemn the world, but that the world through Him might be saved.

MATTHEW 11:28-30

Come to me. all you who labor and are heavy laden, and I will give you rest. Take my yoke upon you and learn from me, for I am gentle and lowly in heart, and you will find rest for your souls. For my yoke is easy and My burden is light.

Nude by Nature

Trust is the foundation of Leadership.

Psalm 139: 13-16-24

For you formed my inward parts,-
You covered me in my mothers womb.
I will praise you, for I am fearfully and wonderfully made.
Marvelous are your works.
And that my soul knows very well.
My frame was not hidden from You when I was made in secret,
And skillfully wrought in the lowest parts of the earth.
Your eyes saw my substance, being yet unformed.
And in Your book they all were written,
The days fashioned for me,
When as yet they were none of them.

How precious also are Your thoughts to me, O God!
How great is the sum of them!
If I should count them, they would be more in number than the sand;
When I awake, I am still with You.

Oh, that You would slay the wicked, O God!
Depart from me, therefore, you bloodthirsty men.
For they speak against You wickedly;
Your enemies take Your name in vain.
Do I not hate them, O Lord, who hate You?

And do I not loathe those who rise up against You?
I hate them with perfect hatred;
I count them my enemies.

Search me, o God, and know my heart,
Try me, and know my anxieties;
And see if there is any wicked way in me,
And lead me in the way everlasting.

ECCLESIASTES 7: 132

For wisdom is a defense as money is a defense,
But the excellence of knowledge – that wisdom gives life to those who have it.

ECCLESIASTES 8:25

I applied my heart to know,
To search and seek out wisdom and the reason of things.

MATTHEW 4:1-11

"It is written man shall not live on bread alone but by every word that proceeds from the mouth of God."

"It is written again: You shall not tempt the Lord your God."

"Away with you, Satan! For it is written: You shall worship the Lord your God, and him only you shall serve."

Then the devil left Him, and behold, angels came and ministered to Him.

James 4:7

Therefore submit to God, Resist the devil and he will flee from you. Draw near to God and He will draw near to you.

James 4: 5-6

Or do you think that the Scripture says in vain, "The spirit who dwells in us yearns jealously"? But He gives more grace. Therefore He says "God resists the proud, But gives grace to the humble."

I see you here, I see you there
I see your soul, laid out bare.
I see the tears hidden away,
I see the hurt, the pain today.
I see the journey taken so far,
I see the impacts, the wounds, the scars,
I see it all laid out there,
I see your soul laid out bare.

I see your pain, I see your loss,
I took it all in an instant upon the cross.
I took it all so that you were free
To live your life, live it free
Be whom I created you to be.
My Son's gift was given freely
Though He paid, He paid dearly.

Suffered through the most enduring pain
By mankind His body slain

Do not let such pain consume you now.
Wipe away your tears, mop your brow.
For freedom came at such a high price.
Paid in full, despite your vice.
For all are tempted, all fall short.
All shall appear at the end in My court.
Judged and tried for what you have done
All forgiven if you have known and loved
My Son.

For Jesus is the way, the truth, the light,
He has carried your sins, won your fight.
So do not let your sins hold you down
any longer.
Turn, repent, deny Satan and grow stronger
For My grace is enough to see you through
Strengthen, soothe your soul, create in you
a new.
A new heart for Jesus, a love for man,
Turn away now, do all you can.

To declare My words, take the ground
Safe in Jesus you will be found.
Loved, secure, ever free
Be the person I created you to be.
Full of hope, purpose, full of joy.
Child of God, girl or boy.
Surrounded in the love of the Father

Receive it now, don't let your heart
grow harder.

Open up your heart, let Me in
To repair and renew, cleansed from sin.
Full of love and hope for man
Love pouring out, do all you can.
To speak My words and declare in My name
Free from guilt, free from shame.
Free to walk in the truth and the light
A beacon of hope to others, a victorious fight.

Safe in the arms of your heavenly Father
Walk in love, walk in peace
Feel My love, it will not cease.
For I AM love, it did not end
Ever present, ready to mend.
Ready to love on those in need
Chains broken, captives freed.
Bondages lifted, hearts open.
Healed by My words, Heaven spoken.

Healed by the work, done on the cross,
You were lifted up; He paid the cost.
To give you life and life in abundance
Bought with love a ransom paid,
For in your hearts He has already made
A way to walk with Him in victory
A way of love poured out so graciously
Poured, overflowing, unending and rich

To bring peace to your soul, pulled from
the ditch.

Washed, renewed, free to be
Righteous, restored, would you walk with Me?
Hold My hand let us walk.
Hold My hand let us talk.
Begin again, fresh and new
Begin again Me and you.
I never left, I never give up.
Ever present, ever ready.

To walk with My children, bound in love.
Watching always from Heaven above.

Deuteronomy 31:6

Be strong and of good courage, do not fear nor be afraid of them; for the Lord your God, is the One who goes with you. He will not leave you nor forsake you."

Deuteronomy 31:8

And the Lord, He is the one who goes before you. He will be with you, He will not lead you nor forsake you, do not fear nor nor be dismayed"

Your mercy, O Lord, is-in the heavens,
Your faithfulness reaches to the clouds.
For with You is the fountain of life,
In Your light we see light.
Hallelujah the trumpets sound.

Come and see

Genesis l: l-5

In the beginning God created the heavens and the earth. The earth was without form, and void: and darkness was on the face of the deep. And the Spirit of God was hovering over the face of the waters. Then God said." Let there be light and there was light. And God saw the light that it was good; and God divided the light from the darkness. God called the light Day, and the darkness He called Night. So the evening and the morning were the first day.

Ever walked in the face of darkness
Ever walked in the face of fear
Ever challenged to say I will succeed
Because you know the Lord is near?

Have you ever seen the light in the darkness
Felt the touch of an angel's wing
Have you ever seen the glory of Heaven
Or the sound when angels sing?

Walk with Me in glorious light
I'll take the blows in the fight.
I'll guide your steps to victory
Separate the darkness from light.

I'll lift you up when you cannot stand
I'll speak when you are silent.

I'll take your pain, I'll give you mercy
Calm the storm when you see only violence

I bring you love, I bring you peace
I bring you Holy victory.
I stand in the void where others fail
I tore the cloth, split the veil.

I do not hide Myself from you
I sent My Son to do what no one could do.
I sent Him down to rescue you.

He broke His heart to rescue yours
He paid the price to open doors
So that man could enter in
Sanctified and free from sin

Redeemed, renewed, all laid bare
Broken down in despair
Lifted up for all to see
Jesus came for victory.

So why the tears, why the cries,
Do not hear the enemies' lies,
Satan was cast down, He was defeated
Read My Word, do not be cheated.

Satan was beaten at the cross
Eternally defeated, such a loss
For though he was the morning star
He thirst glory, thirst for power

And this leads to pride and death within.
This leads to arrogance, a deadly sin.
When love is lost and love cast out
Death enters in, its fear will shout.

"I cannot love an empty heart,
I cannot give to those who are weak,
I cannot love those you seek."

But My love gives to all in need
My love gives to all who are freed.
Free from sin, free in Him
Declared salvation is where it is to begin

Declared as Your Lord and Saviour
Receive Christ now, change your behaviour
Light comes in, darkness leaves,
Love moves into your heart to receive

The Holy Spirit, a gift from me
Your eternal helper, brings victory.
Love in the darkest corner of life
Love to a husband and a wife

Love to the widow, grieving the loss
Love to the soul, counting the cost
Love to the tender hearts so young
Love to the broken, healing has begun.

Love in the darkness, separated from light.
Love endures all, victory is won

Love in its purest form,
Love from My Son.

So open up, come and see
Feel the glory of victory
Feel My love, free your pain
When darkness flees, you have much to gain

Sanctified, redeemed, cleansed, reborn
The Saviour's love you now adorns
Clothed in the love never to be lost
My son gave you it all when he died on
the cross.

Freed from sin, enter My grace
Set apart in the holy place
Ready to walk in victory.
Ready to feel what your eyes cannot see.

For no one knows what I have planned
No one knows what lies ahead
The new life has come,
The old is dead.

So take a step and walk with Me
Walk the path of victory.
Free from sin, free to breathe
The light is here, darkness must leave.

Pain and suffering left behind
Lies removed, no longer blind

Victorious in the Father's love
Called down to earth from Heaven above

Called to all who accept My Son
Welcomed home, in Him your new life
has begun.

Jeremiah 29: Il-13

For I know the thoughts that I think toward you, says the Lord, thoughts of peace and not evil, to give you a future and a hope.

l Samuel 16:7

"But the Lord said to Samuel, Look not on his appearance or at the height of his stature, for I have rejected him. For the Lord sees not as man sees; for man looks on the outward appearance, but the Lord looks on the heart.

John 3:16

For God so loved the world that he gave His only begotten son, that whoever believes in Him should not perish but have everlasting life. For God did not send His Son into the world to condemn the world, but that the world through Him might be saved.

Romans 10:9

If you confess with your mouth the Lord Jesus and believe in your heart that God has raised Him from the dead, you will be saved. For with the heart one believes unto righteousness, and with the mouth confession is made unto salvation. For the scripture says, "whoever believes on Him will not be put shame." For there no distinction between Jew and Greek, for the same Lord overall is rich to all who call upon Him. For "Whoever calls on the name of the Lord shall be saved."

Andrew's Benediction

Your Promises define me.
Lift our heads to see you.

SANCTIFICATION

Sanctification:
The outworking of the Holy Spirit in the believer's life. The state or process of being, set apart, sacred purpose, to make holy or sacred, cooperation with God to be made holy as a vessel full of the Holy Spirit of God.

Prophetic Image inspired by Psalm 150:6 "Let everything that has breath praise the Lord, Praise the Lord" NKJV

The artwork shows the viewer how praise and worship connect mankind with our heavenly Father. When we take our focus off ourselves and our problems and give thanks to God through praise and worship, we realign our priorities and restore our souls. The artwork shows the many facets of praise and worship, what it means to the person giving thanks to God, how we can find rest during the process, and how God uses it to minister to us. The scripture reference within the time signature (150/6) refers to the appointed time in the purpose of God, the Kairos. The musical "repeat" symbol represents the need for Humanity to continually repeat praise and worship in all seasons of life.

The microphone, central to the image, represents the tree of knowledge and the tree of good and evil. Songs are used to speak life into situations, for breakthrough, praise and worship. The fruit coming off the tree is the musical notes that are coloured according to the colours of the rainbow, representing God's promises being received and spoken out through the atmosphere. The low hanging fruit are the "sub-whole notes" with the "full note" raising up into the third heaven where the Arc of the Covenant is. The musical "staff" represents the book of names and the songs already written in heaven that will be sung on earth and in heaven. The symbol of the "sharp" represents the major key as the musical locksmith opening up hearts to receive and give out worship.

The tree is situated at the edge of the river where it draws its life from the living water, Jesus Christ. The coloured bands around the tree trunk represent the relationship of Jesus (Purple), Mankind (Red) and the Holy Spirit (Blue). The foreground rocks in the stream represent the keys worn-out during our current circumstance. At times we can be worn down by our own circumstances; we need to realise that singing songs of praise and worship can bring positive change and hope for a better future. As we look to the source of our living water (Jesus), we see perfection and clear unworn keys moving upwards in the distance.

The landscape shows the earth, second heaven and third heaven. God's promises, represented by the rainbow, are kept regardless of the blue skies of summer or the dark skies of winter.

As we move through the landscape we can see and experience rest (as in the musical symbol representation) in all its forms. These are places of shelter but not permanent places to stay. Short rests are often taken when things look good, but are not permanent. As you move closer to submission, you experience a deeper rest and a closer relationship with our Father, as seen by the symbolic "half rests" in the riverbed. The riverbed is dry and without the water needed. Full rest is found when we submit during our trials. This is represented by the person on their knees submitted to God. The "bass clef" (low notes) demonstrate total submission as we praise and worship the father – the contrast of earthly submission to Heavenly adoration.

Ask yourself the following questions:

What does sanctification mean to me?

Do I believe it? If not why not?

What does the bible say?

What actions can I take to change this mindset?

What action will I take to change this mindset?

Speak to the Lack, Speak Life

Psalm 36:7-9

How precious is Your loving kindness Oh God!
Therefore the children of men put their trust under the shadow of Your wings.
They are abundantly satisfied with the fullness of Your house
And You give them drink from the river of Your pleasures.
For with You is the fountain of life,
In Your light we see light.

As the world was created, so was man.
Through the power of My voice, so your world is located.
Your challenges overcome
You must always make a choice
Do you accept what is?
Do you walk in fear?
Do you hang your head down low?
Do you walk in shame?
Are you physically lame?
Do you even know which way to go?

You have a voice, you have a choice
To call upon your Heavenly Father.
For I am here, I am near,
Waiting to rush in with love.
Call to Me, come be here
From earthly toils and pain.

I am here for you,
I am here with you.
Let us walk out over the plains.

In victory we stand
By the power of My hand
The love of My Son, Jesus Christ
For what He did at the cross.
Paid for your loss,
So that you could live a victorious life
So walk out in strength
With provision Heaven sent
To a victorious land so rich
Where your children will grow
Where your family will sow
An abundant blessing to all.

For you answered My call.
I won't let you fall.
I will hold you and guide your steps.
I will show you how.
I will show you now.
Come follow Me, Jesus said.
Lay down your nets,
Lay down your lives.

Live in Me and with Me today.
Speak out My words to the multitude of hearts,
Lambs a plenty to save.
For they all need love,

They all need care, the word of the
Gospel heals.
So speak to them now,
Speak to them here,
Speak the words of Heaven.
Speak to your lack,
Speak to your battle,
Call the victory now.
Call down your angels,
Call down your blessings,
Call down your Father's love.

Call to Me and you will see.
There is nothing I cannot fix.
For I am created with word
This is what you have heard
Now speak and behold with your heart.

Your voice has power
Your voice has strength
You voice is the spirit of God
So speak out to all
Let them answer My call
Free them from bondages and sin
For Christ is our Saviour.
Christ is our Lord.
He died to set you free,
He comes in love,
He comes in truth
He came to save humanity.

He came for you, He came for all
Was such a gift from God.
A gift brings pleasure,
A gift brings joy,
A gift so rare and precious.
Receive it now, receive the love
The Father's joy called down from above.
Breathe it in, wrap it around.
In Christ we trust, in Christ we are found.

Psalm 36:5

Your mercy O Lord, is in the heavens
Your faithfulness reaches to the clouds.

John 14:27

Peace I leave with you, My peace I give to you not as the world gives do I give to you. Let not your heart be troubled, neither let it be afraid.

Bathed in Love

Psalm 40:2

He brought me up out of the pit of destruction, out of the miry clay,
And He set my feet upon a rock making my footsteps firm.

Isaiah 43:2

When you pass through the waters, I will be with you; And through the rivers, they will not overflow you when you walk through the fire, you will not be scorched, nor the flame burn you.

Jeremiah 29:11

For I know the plans I have for you, declares the Lord, plans for welfare and not for evil, to give you a future and a hope.

Isaiah 40:31

But they who wait for the Lord shall renew their strength; they shall mount up with wings like eagles; they shall run and not be weary; they shall walk and not faint.

Bathed in love, a gift from above
For a price you did not pay.
Bought with His blood,
A ransom of love
For all to receive each day.

Pour out your heart,
Bring peace to your soul
Hand over your sorrow and pain.
Let Me cover you in love
Called down from above
To protect you and remove your shame.

I know your heart,
I know your soul.
The peace and joy I will restore
For this life is short.
The heavy price you were bought
There is no time to waste in regrets.

Lift up your heart
Receive a fresh start
Through Christ your redeemer, your King.
For all have fallen short
All have sinned
Yet Jesus all these He has overcome.

Bathe in My love
A gift from above
Let me restore what was taken away.
Together we walk
Together we talk
Let us journey together in love.

I know your heart
I've known from the start
I placed these gifts in you

So open your mind, for the Saviour kind,
Mercy and love of the Father.

I want to begin, now you are washed of
your sin
In a pasture so fresh and clear.
So take up your pen, let us begin
Write down the things that you hear.

For all fall short
All have sinned
All have some kind of need
And though they may hear
Some still fear the judgement and scorn of man.
But what can he do, for if only he knew,
The power of the blood of the Lamb.

To clean and restore
Their sins on the floor
Broken and wasted away
So speak out this love
From the Father above
Let them hear My words wash over them
And then they will see, the love I gave thee,
A love that cleanses all
A love so true
A love redeemed you
Bought at the price of My Son.

So sing out My name
And above all I reign

So come to the Father in love
I will not turn away
Any who say, I repent, help me I'm lost.
For you were bought at a price
Of value to me, I will not let any fall down.
For the Father is loving, He calls you by name
He renews the hardest of hearts.
So come to Him now, let us begin
Bathe in His love, wash away your sin
Through the blood of His Son, Jesus Christ.

He will cleanse you within
He will love you throughout
He will restore that which is lost
He will renew your mind
Through the scriptures he will bind
The demons who chase you down.

Be strong in My Word
Declare with your mouth
And satan will flee your land
For the Word is the sword
And faith is the shield
I have put these in your hand.

Take to your mountain
Renew strength in My fountain,
Bathe in My love for you
And together we march
To the valleys of peace
To the ground I have promised you.

Stand strong in the Word
Declare what you have heard
And see the armies flee
For the army of truth
Greater at youth, will overcome the lies
and doubt.
Declare My love
Sing My praise
I will walk with you
All of your days

Through the valleys low, the mountains high
Glorious music will fill the sky
Sing out to the Lord
Know you are called
For battles I have won

Raise up and march
To the land I declared
Take all that I have given you
Be strong to sing
Be wise to learn
Be open to My words.

And onwards we will march
To victorious lands
Praises will be sung
To the heavens above
Praises heard of God's true love
Praise to God the most high.
Praise to the King, praise we will sing

Bathed in the love of His Son
Bathed in the love, passed down from above
Bathed in His righteousness.

MATTHEW 16:18 - 19

"And I say to you that you are Peter, and on this rock I will build My church, and the gates of Hades shall not prevail against it. And I will give you the keys of the Kingdom of heaven, and whatever you bind on earth will be bound in heaven, and whatever you loose on earth will be loosed in heaven."

Encouragement

Samuel 16:11-13

And Samuel said to Jesse, "Are all the young men here?" Then he said, "There remains yet the youngest, and there he is, keeping the sheep." And Samuel said to Jesse, "Send and bring him. For we will not sit down till he comes here." So he sent and brought him in. Now he was ruddy, with bright eyes, and good-looking. And the Lord said, "Arise, anoint him, for this is the one!" Then Samuel took the horn of oil and anointed him in the midst of his brothers, and the Spirit of the Lord came upon David from that day forward. So Samuel arose and went to Ramah.

The face in a crowd,
Doesn't have to speak loud.
For the voice you have heard
Is the promise of My Word.

The time in your life
To find a husband or wife
Is a time so precious to Me.
For deep in your heart is where I look,
To reveal the seeds you sow from My book.

To open a chapter, to close a verse.
To speak to a nation or charge forward
from reverse.
Seek My counsel and open your heart,

Allow My words to penetrate your heart.
Allow your eyes to see from within the crowd.
Hear the roar of the Spirit, so quiet, so loud.
Reverent and loving, careful and true,
The Holy Spirit My gift to you.

Help Me to help you,
Each and every way.
The words to speak, so much to say.
Where you walk and what you see.
Allow My Spirit to speak to thee.

Open your eyes and behold wonderful things
Hear My voice, oh how My Spirit sings.
Loud and royal, oh heavenly voice,
Love of the Father, heavens rejoice.
Cherished and loved, oh My beautiful Son,
Sacrificed and reborn to restore the One.

The one today and yesterday
The one tomorrow, here and now.
The one to come, the one who has been,
Each one I love, each one I have seen.
So walk with me in all you do.
Walk with Me, I walk with you.

Genesis 2:9

Then the Lord God called to Adam and said to him, "Where are you?"

Psalm 119:105

Your word is a lamp for my feet, a light on my path.

Peace I bring to you

Peace I bring to you
Not as the world sees but as I reveal to you.
Peace in your heart.
Peace in your mind
Peace that only My Spirit can define.

It cannot be bought,
It cannot be given,
It comes from within,
Through the Holy Spirit given.
The perfect gift in the perfect season,
Holy in love,
Heavenly reason.

I give to you now, so that you must say,
Remember your gift, I remember the day.
It was not special, but we were alone,
No interruptions, no one on the phone.
You welcomed me in, into your home.
Into your life, your thoughts, your heart.
Deep in your hidden man,
Where no one can see.
A spot I created, specifically for Me.

That you would know when I arrived.
To give you peace, as your old self died.
Born again, spirit renewed,
Negativity gone, depression refused.

For a new creation you are
With life and purpose
Gifted in love, let My gifts come to service
Free to all who come to Me.
Visions of life, what do you see?

Do you see the beauty on a flower's petal?
Or the rain falling down, dripping off metal.
Pastures green or brambles bare.
Beauty refined if you would only stare.

Stirred in creation, souls to meet.
Divine connections, oil to your feet.
Perfumed from Heaven
Clothed in love
Came down from Heaven
In the form of a dove.
Gentle and powerful
Strong and refined.
Eyes now open, never blind.

Free to look and free to see.
All I have I give to thee.
Heaven called down to touch the earth,
The ultimate sacrifice, the miracle birth.

All that has happened and all that is to come.
I give you My peace, from father to son.
Mother to daughter, the Holy one.

Take My hand and walk a while.
Gently meander, like the Nile.
Over land and rivers deep.
Ask and you shall find Me,
Promises I keep.

Promises to guide you on your way.
Promises spoken, words to say.
Dreams to fulfil and dreams to share.
Oh how I love you, Oh how I care.

So take this step and hold My hand.
Together we will walk across the land.
Taking dominion of all that is yours.
Walking in favour, grace and laws.

Fixed meetings and divine encounters,
Places to be, a moment in time.
Specific relationships, so complete, so divine.
Souls to meet, souls to entwine.

Purposed for glory and praise to your Father.
Walk in My Spirit, further and further.
Deeper and deeper into waters unknown
Eternally linked to your heavenly home.

Peace and abundance, love and pleasure.
Relationship with the Father,
A heavenly treasure.

So walk ahead, don't look back.
Spread out My scriptures and feed your future.
Walk with and listen to My worthy teacher.
For the Spirit walks to bring about My will.
He wants to help you over this hill.

Onto the next one, and then over that.
Uphill, downhill even on the flat.
For all of life, He is ever present.
Gifted by Me, Heaven sent.
To teach you, to love you, to open your eyes.
To dream and fulfil,
Dream up in the skies.
To call down Heaven to touch the earth.
To bring about love,
Ideas birthed.

Talk with Me, and walk with Me,
I will show you the way.
Listen to My Spirit, deep in your heart.
For Jesus died to give you new life.
Jesus died to bring you peace.
Jesus died so that you were released.
Released from sin and free to love.
Baptised in My Spirit,
The gift from above.

Use My Spirit to bring about change.
Through Jesus Christ, the beautiful exchange.
Peace and love I bring to thee.
The Father's gift, a gift from Me.

JOHN 1:32

And John bore witness, saying, "I saw the Spirit descending from heaven like a dove and He remained upon Him."

MATTHEW 3:16

When He had been baptized, Jesus came up immediately from the water; and behold, the heavens were opened to Him, and He saw the Spirit of God descending like a dove and alighting upon Him.

Declaration of God's love

2 Samuel 7:26

So let your name be magnified forever, saying, "The Lord of hosts is the God over Israel."

Deep in the heart is where I start,
When I look for someone like Me.
Deep in the mind, is where you will find the
secret to unlock My key.
Buried in scripture, revealed in light,
Heaven on earth is where we will fight.
Declaring the future, living the now,
Forgetting the past each day.
Open your bible, pray in tongues,
Listen to what I have to say.
For Jesus is King, Lord of all things,
Nothing will stand in My way.

Open your mouth, declare through your soul,
Enriched and enlightened in Christ.
For though you are small,
In Me you are tall,
Nothing is too far gone to renew.

I made you in love, a gift from above.
Defined to achieve great things.
So why do you mope?
Look to Me in hope.
Faith in your Heavenly Father above.

I called you out.
I knew you inside.
With Me you are safe,
Nothing to hide.

I know your pain,
It will won't always remain, in the flesh it can be overtaken.
But that day on the cross,
When Jesus paid the cost.
It was for then, now and forever.

So in Christ you are free.
Through My grace to thee.
Don't let the enemy tell you different.

For he would if he could.
Make you look back over your past.
Your present and future.

But only I know.
Over which path you will go.
Sanctified, righteous in Me.

So don't think for a minute.
That you cannot win it.
This battle ground you stand in alone.
My hand is wide,
Protector, comforter, guide.
So declare with your mouth,
The victory is given.

In Christ you achieve all.
For after death he was risen.

To show the world My truth.
From baby to youth
To present and latter years.

It will not be taken, My promises spoken,
Over you and all that is to come.
So smile and move on.
Your sin is undone.
There is joy in the world.
Now is the time to have fun.

Open your eyes,
To My daily surprise.
Life is abundant with love.

Love is endured.
Love is never ignored.
It breaks the hardest of hearts.
Love can redeem, if you are willing to glean,
The wonders inside My Word.

For I am love.
I am above.
I cover you in blessings today.
And though you don't see.
My hand over thee,
Be still and know that I am here.

For I will not go.
And leave you in woe.
I am your Father in Heaven.
And though it seems hard.
To be dealt such a card.
I know it is good for your soul.

For out of the pit.
Is where you will sit.
At the right hand of the Father.
In Jesus you are frce.
Sat next to Me.
You don't have to work any harder.

I loved you in Heaven.
I love you now.
I love you always, eternal.
Be courageous and strong.
You are where you belong.
Never ever be fearful.

For yes and amen, are the promises to you.
In truth and in love, do all that you do.
And know that your past is past.

A new day has come.
A new song to be sung.
The joy of salvation is here.

So step out in love.
Step out in Christ.

God bless you, In Christ we live.
God bless you in Christ we live.

JEREMIAH 33:1-3

Moreover the word of the Lord came to Jeremiah a second time, while he was still shut up in the court of the prison, saying, "Thus says the Lord who made it, the Lord who formed it to establish, (The Lord is His name): "Call to Me, and I will answer you, and show you great and mighty things which you do not know."

AMOS 9:11

On that day I will raise up the tabernacle of David, which has fallen down, and repair its damages. I will raise up its rains, and rebuild it as in the days of old."

LUKE 1:37

For no word from God will ever fail.

Reflections of You

Reflections of you is all I can do,
When I'm limited by myself.
I look in my eyes, see fire and ice.
Burnt out misery, no wealth.
Invested in me I cannot see
The reason to go on ahead.
For each day I arise
To the demon's surprise
He's here and I feel dead.

For I have nothing to give
Nor do I feel I should live
When all seems lost and forgotten.
How do I fly when I feel I should die
For the sins are too much to bear.

Who do I call, when I get up from the fall?
The dark secrets with someone to share.
Then all of a sudden
I'm no longer downtrodden.
I rise from the ashes of hell.
For none can see me.
Except the Almighty
Who wraps me in His arms of love.
For now I see why I had to cry
Help me Abba Father, help me.

For though I am lost.
You paid the cost
Redeemed me so long ago.
For I am victorious in love.
From My Father above.
Who gave His own Son for me.

So how can I share the loss of despair
If My Father has taken it at the cross?
For I have been forgiven
When Christ was risen
And healed me before I was born.

The enemy's lies, should come as no surprise
For a thief and a liar he is.
And free that I am
To stand in the land
To share Christ's love to all.
So come to the Father
Do not despair
For the Father's love is for all.

And rise I must,
In Him I trust.
To free me from pain and sin.
So though I may cry
I will not die
For eternity starts at the cross.

Forgiven in truth
The old and the youth.

Timeless in our deity
For Christ is the King
In Him we must sing
Halleluiah Emmanuel.
Halleluiah Emmanuel.
Halleluiah we sing
Halleluiah Emmanuel.

Carrying the mantle

1 Thessalonians 1:5-6

For our gospel did not come to you in word only, but also in power, and in the Holy Spirit and in much assurance, as you know what kind of men were among you for your sake.
And you became followers of us and of the Lord, having received the word in much affliction, with joy of the Holy Spirit, so that you became examples to all in Macedonia and Achaia who believe.

1 Peter 2:9

But you are a chosen generation, a royal priesthood, a holy nation, His own special people, that you may proclaim the praises of Him who called you out of darkness into His marvellous light:

Vision of a child carrying an American football under his arm. He is the quarterback. Protected by the pack at all costs but carries the most important asset – the Word of God. Not known for physical size or strength but known for carrying, sending and receiving the message of hope, the message of Christ.

Vision of the parents standing at an elevated position looking out over a vast land, happy that the mantle has been passed on. Looking out through glass windows.

Oh how the foolish do not see.
The plans of prosperity I have for thee.
The plans to grow My kingdom far.
Plans to reach beyond the stars.
Plans of hope of families lost,
A place to stay without the cost.
A place of safety when all is gone,
Secured and loved just like My Son.

I have called what is not yet seen,
A testimony of vision,
If you would only lean.
Lean on Me and in Me,
I will not forsake.
Heaven's journey, if you would partake,
Fields of living water wide,
Love running over, far and wide.

I will share My heart with you alone,
Safe in the security of your home.
Safe in the love of mum and dad,
Knowing you are here but you never had.
The chance to speak so clear and true,
But now My love will show through you.

For I have called you to speak My words,
I have chosen you to manage My herds.
The little shepherd boy over looked,

Yet now we know he is in The Book.
The little shepherd boy, meek and mild,
The little shepherd boy, God's anointed child.

I have chosen men from hearts,
I have chosen love hidden deep.
I have chosen those who would speak,
The scripture heard, My laws to keep.
For man cannot live on bread alone,
Man must build himself a home.

Safe and secure on Heaven's foundation.
Safe in My Love, speaking without hesitation.
My words will be heard through the voice of
your child.
Gentle and loving, meek and mild.
Do not think your child has no knowledge,
For he has begun to use his voice,
He will guide you to make the right choice.

For love is pure, love is true,
My gift of a child I give to you.
Nurture his heart, nurture his speech,
Educated and confused he will teach.
All about the love of Christ.
Simple and true, honest and brave,
Many a soul he will save.

I placed him in your special care,
Safe in the family, rooted there.
Secure in love to grow and mature,

A seasoned vine, true and pure.
Loved and loving so gentle a soul,
Fills the darkest, tired hole.
With love and words so open and true,
My gift of love, My gift to you.
So watch and nurture this boy's heart,
Riches will pour out of his loving heart.
Riches you cannot yet openly see,
Riches I have planted, in him for thee.

I blessed you going out, and coming in,
Abundant blessing about to begin.
Watch his heart open and wide,
Love poured out it cannot hide.
Love so powerful, it pours far and wide,
Love in abundance for all mankind.

Love to all of humanity,
Love I give you through him, from Me.
Love is our greatest gift.
Love heals any rift.
Love unites and ties together.
A family unit loved forever.
Loved as one, lived as many.
Love cherished, love protected.
Love as Christ does, resurrected.

Out of pain, beauty arisen,
Love pierces the darkest prison.
Love is celebrated far and wide.
Love in light, darkness cannot hide.

Love poured out for all to see.
The love I have I give to thee.
Love so perfect it cannot be taken,
Love of My children never forsaken.

Love is pure, love is true,
This love I give, I give to you.
Peace and love we give to children
Yet they give us so much more in return.

Matthew 18:1-5

At that time the disciples came to Jesus, saying, "Who then is greatest in the kingdom of heaven?" Then Jesus called a little child to Him, set him in the midst of them, and said, "Assuredly, I say to you, unless you are converted and become as little children, you will by no means enter the kingdom of heaven. Therefore who ever humbles himself as this little child is greatest in the kingdom of heaven. Whoever receives one little child like this in My name receives Me.

Psalm 127:3-5

Behold, children are a heritage from the Lord, The fruit of the womb is a reward.
Like arrows in the hand of a warrior,
So are the children of one's youth.
Happy is the man who has his quiver full of them;
They shall not be ashamed,
But shall speak with their enemies in the gate.

You lead we stand

A PRAYER when faced with adversity.
When the light is pushing back the dark but we feel the darkness is pushing back on us.
God is victorious.
Jesus is our Lord and Saviour.
The Holy Spirit is our advocate.

Don't lose the eternal perspective.
Flesh Vs Spiritual

Ephesians 2:2-4

In which you were once walked according to the course of this world, according to the prince of the power of the air, the spirit who now works in the sons of disobedience, among whom also we all once conducted ourselves in the lusts of our flesh, fulfilling the desires of the flesh and of the mind, and were by nature children of wrath, just as the others. But God, who is rich in mercy, because of His great love with which He loved us,"

Romans 10:12-21

For there is no distinction between Jew and Greek, for the same Lord over all is rich to all who call upon Him, "For whoever calls on the name of the Lord shall be saved." How then shall they call on Him in whom they have not believed? And how shall they believe in Him of whom they have not heard? And

how shall they hear without a preacher? And how shall they preach unless they are sent? As it is written:
"How beautiful are the feet of those who preach the gospel of peace, Who bring glad tidings of good things!"
But they have not all obeyed the gospel. For Isaiah says, "LORD, who has believed our report? So then faith comes by hearing, and hearing by the word of God. But I say, have they not heard? Yes indeed:
"Their sound has gone out to all the earth, And their words to the ends of the world."
But I say, did Israel not know? First Moses says:
"I will provoke you to jealousy by those who are not a nation, I will move you to anger by a foolish nation, But Isaiah is very bold and says:
I was found by those who did not seek me, I was made manifest to those who did not ask for Me." But Israel he says:
All day long I have stretched out My hands
To disobedient and contrary people."

You lead, we stand, Lord you're beautiful.
Lord you're beautiful.
You reach, guide our hand
Lord you're wonderful
Lord you're wonderful.

You speak, we hear
Your voice, so magical
So magical.
We see your love

Praise and honour you
Praise and honour you

Spirit of God, Father and Son
Lord you are one and all
You are one and all.

Fill up our hearts
Take us in Your hands
Guide us on our path
Make us strong in faith.
Make us strong in faith.

Jesus, Jesus
You died for me on that cursed tree.
Raised up from death
You were born again.
Born to set me free
For all eternity.

Spirit of God, Father and the Son,
You are one and all
You are one and all.

Shining down your light
Mercy oh so bright.
You are Lord of all.
You are Lord of all.

Hear our prayers tonight
Help us stand the fight.

For the battle's Yours
We stand for the cause.

Heal our souls
Deliver our foes.
Righteous and just
In You we trust.

Spirit of God
Father and the Son
You are one and all
You are Lord of all.

I will sing

My soul will sing with a heart of desire,
To know you Lord,
To know you Lord.

I will lift my arms to My Lord and King
To the one who lives,
To the Lord we sing.

And my soul will know how You love me so,
How my heart lights up in the afterglow.

Oh my soul will sing
How I love You so
How I love You more
As I raise my hands
To the One I adore.

I lift them up as a sign of love
To the one true God
Our Father in Heaven above.
I hear Your cry as the lion roars,
I hear Your cry as the eagle soars.
As my heart grows strong
I hear the sound of the angels' roar,
As they cry out Lord to the One adored.
Seated on high, Hallelujah.

Lay it down

Laid down bare where my words cannot go
Laid out on the line with nothing more to show.
Will I feel the same again?
Will I love myself anymore?
Laid down at the cross, Will He open the door?

Will He speak, will He listen?
Will He comfort or rage?
I have nothing to bargain with, deep within
my cage.
For bars surround me, I cannot break free.
I only see death of what I could be.

I see destruction, the broken hearted.
My words and actions, friends dearly departed.
I hate the existence my life has become.
No longer loved, completely undone.

But here in the moment the daylight breaks
The Heavens are roaring, my prison shakes.
My Saviour has heard me, He knows my name,
He comes with a fire, my soul is reclaimed.

For righteous and justice His character is true.
He comes to bring love poured out over you.
Washed over in love, the greatest of gifts.
My soul is replenished, the darkness it lifts.

The light breaks through the darkest of hours
The pain washed away in the heavenly showers
The richness of love washes the soul
The greatest love fills the darkest hole.
Pain and suffering all undone.
Rebuilt and renewed, in the name of His Son.

Refreshed by grace in a moment of time
The Shepherd knows his sheep
And you are Mine.
So do not believe the lics and the doubt.
For Heaven angels roar, Hallelujah they shout.

Praise be to the Father, His kingdom is here.
Praise to the Father, ever loving, so near.
So near and pure, He is love itself.
Through all things He will endure,
His righteousness our wealth.

So lift up your heart, let the angels hear
you sing.
Poured down from Heaven, His blessings
they sing.
Rich in beauty, rich in love.
The greatest gift, from your Father in
Heaven above.

You speak to my heart, you release my mind.
In you I trust, in you I find.
The love and the courage to bring love to bare.
My Father sees me, He shows me he cares.

He cares so much He gave His Son.
A beautiful exchange, our battles He won.
So when the enemy comes at our mind,
Declare the scriptures and protect our mind.
Protect our heart from the lies of the thief.
Step out of the cage into the Father's relief.

Relief to breathe, relief to love.
Enveloped in love from our Father above.
Free to live in all that we can be.
Our eyes are opened, now we can see.
See the riches from our Father in Heaven.
Restored and rebuilt, our loss times seven.

Complete in love, beauty abound.
Safe in the Father's arms, is where we
are found.
No longer trapped in a cage so tight.
The darkness is driven away, let there be light.

Let there be light in all that we see.
Love of Jesus set the captives free.
Free to love, free to believe.
Freely given, freely received.

Receive the gift from a Father's love.
Poured out on mankind from Heaven above.
Poured out in righteousness, love abound.
Christ victorious, in Him we are found.

Reputation

God builds character ready for His story to unfold. Man creates heroic characters in a make-believe story. God builds character in lives to carry out heroic acts. In movies heroes are worshipped. In faith, humble people worship God. Heroes have a passion for the cause. In faith, God is the cause and He gives you the passion.

Do not fear the path of your life,
for I have chosen your perfect wife.
To come together hand in hand,
to walk together across the land.
Over seas and kingdoms wide,
there is no place where My love will hide.
For I have given you My Spirit of love,
I have sent Him down from above.
To release the captives, redeem the lost.
Break the bondages no matter the cost.

I will endure until the end,
I will strengthen you, protect My friend.
For I have chosen the steps you walk,
I have given you the words to talk.
To remove the armies standing in your way,
to go forward from this day.
Do not stop, do not faulter,
for your life you laid down at the altar.

Forgiveness and love are My rewards,
In peoples' hearts this will pull on their chords.
To bring them back to Me once more,
to call them forward across the shore.
Across the storms that they face,
to a safe haven, a heavenly place.
Free from guilt and free from sin,
free from bondages held within.
So speak out truth, speak out love,
speak the words from your heavenly
Father above.
Speak My love to the lost and found,
speak My Word to all around.

Speak to the nations bold and true,
speak the words I give to you.
Speak the truth, the light and the way,
people will listen to the words you say.

Believe in Me, for I am within you,
watch the miracles I create through you.
Watch redemption come to pass,
watch the healings ever last.
Watch the love people will feel,
broken hearts start to heal.
Relationships restored and new ones formed,
Christ in glory, His love adorned.
Be pure in heart and mercy full,
love poured out, your cup so full.

That all may drink and never thirst,
all may quench the ache they feel.
All drink from Me and fill their hearts,
with My love, a new fresh start.
Redeemed in My love, sanctified, reborn,
purpose driven with love from Heaven.
Walking in life with the power of the cross,
restored through Jesus, all that was lost.
Be strong and courageous, full of faith,
I am with you to bring about restoration.

I am the King of Kings, Lord of lords,
I am here, there, all over,
I am therefore and I will, and I have,
I am love, truth, kindness, peace, joy, happiness

Exodus 3:14

And God said to Moses, "I AM WHO I AM" and He said, "This you shall say to the children of Isreal, I AM has sent me to you." Moreover God said to Moses, " This you shall say to the children of Israel: "The Lord God of your Fathers, the God of Abraham, the God of Isaac and the God of Jacob, has sent me to you. This is My name forever, and this is why memorial to all the generations

Exodus 3:16

"I have surely visited you and seen what is done to you in Egypt; "I have said I will bring you up out of the afflictions of Egypt. "To a land flowing of milk and honey."

Luke 7:22-23

Are you him or should we look for another? "Then Jesus answering said unto them, "Go your way, and tell John what things ye have seen and heard; how the blind see, how the lame walk, the dead are raised, to the poor the gospel is preached. Are blessed is he, whosoever shall not be offended in me

Luke 7:50

And he said to the woman, "Thy faith hath saved thee, go in peace."

2 Samuel 6:19

So David inquired of the Lord, saying, "Shall I go up against the Philistines? Will You deliver them into my hand?" And the law said to David, "Go, up, for a doubtless deliver the Philestines into your hand."

A Warrior's Call

Isaiah 13:3

I have commanded My sanctified ones;
I have also called My mighty ones for My anger.
Those who rejoice in My exaltation.

I have seen the eyes of hate,
I have seen the eyes of love.
I have seen hell fire brought down from above.
A scorched place so barren and cold,
Green valleys and hills to welcome me home.
A sky so bright I cannot hide
The crest of a wave as I surf the tide.
The touch on my shoulder to know I must go,
The pain of the journey some may never know.
But most would say that you look well,
Even after closing the door on hell.
Mateship and friendship, open arms,
A hand to hold as you touch each other's palms.
For love can bring blue skies to storms,
A gentle breath as your insides warm.
You walk in freedom around your home.
Knowing that you are never alone.
Yet some may fall because demons chase,
You stand in victory by His Lord's grace.
And as you shine the smile of joy.
Surrounded in love, girl and boy.
Friendship, mateship, one true love.
Crowned in compassion from above.

Reach out your hand to those in need,
Destroy their demons, show them how to lead.
And by the grace of God walk tall,
Testimony of righteousness, one and all.

Keep moving forward with love and laughter as you show others how to heal.

Proverbs 23:10-11

If you faint in the day of adversity, your strength is small. Deliver those who are drawn towards death. And hold back those stumbling to the slaughter.

PROMISE

Promise:
A gracious gift from God to the believer.

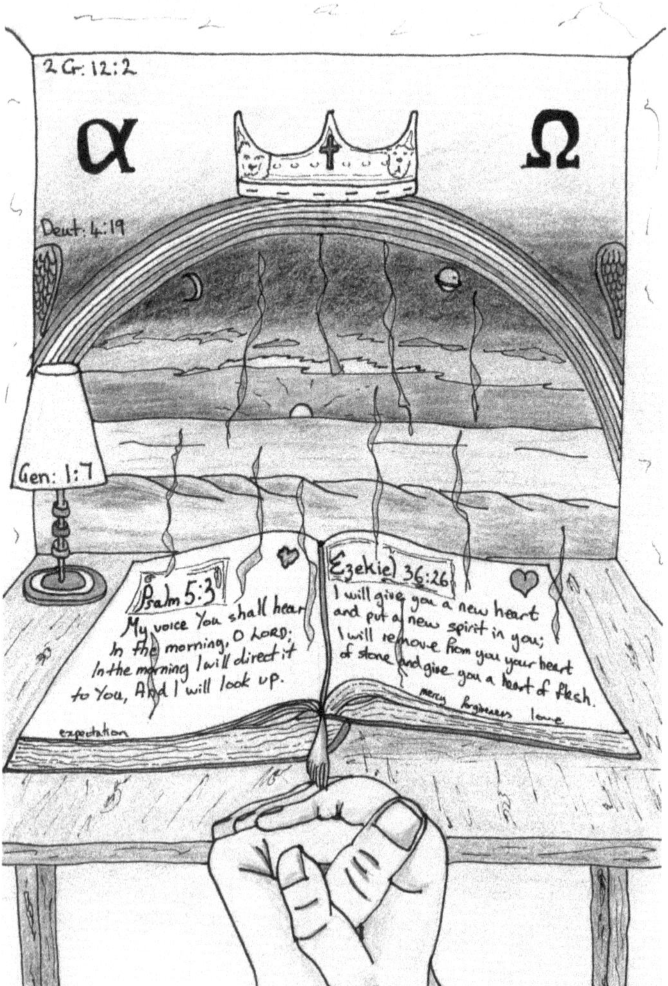

Promises of God

The image portrays the journey of prayer - from the hands held together symbolically as a person praying, to the third heaven activation shown above the horizon and beyond the natural skyline. It is a call to action from our Father in heaven to the listener. Whether praying for your own circumstance or someone else's, the image demonstrates the direct connection between the earthly dimension of physical hands, through the written scripture, to the spiritual realms of heaven beyond the depth of the page. The promises of God represented by the rainbow highlight the eternal relationship God has with man, and the promises He swore to keep after the great flood to the very end of time. His sovereign control of all things is depicted by the King's crown with the symbolic lion and lamb drawn to identify the role of Christ within the Godhead. He is a living sacrificial lamb and the roaring lion of Judah. Jesus sits as King wearing the crown, spanning across all time from beginning to end. The bible is open to these particular scriptures which show the relationship of praying to our Father in heaven. Through this relational interaction we are transformed into a new creation over time. The rainbow bookmark represents the promises found in scripture.

In the foreground is a table emphasizing the importance of having a place to pray, just as God has set a table for us to feast on His love. Early in the morning is quite often a good time to pray, as we have not been bombarded with the world and its trials. We step out into our day on the front foot, filled with confidence in our Lord God in heaven and daily strengthening our relationship with Him.

Psalm 5:3.

My voice You shall hear in the morning, O Lord;
In the morning I will direct it to You,
And I will look up.

We are expectant as we speak with our Father in heaven. The purple heart represents Jesus waiting to talk with us as we look up to heaven. The red heart represents our earthly, stony heart receiving mercy, forgiveness and love from heaven, which transforms the heart of stone into a new heart of flesh. No matter what your current circumstance, God offers you a fresh start.

Ezekiel 36:26

I will give you a new heart and put a new spirit within you; I will take the heart of stone out of your flesh and give you a heart of flesh.

The purple flames are the anointed words of power that are released as we read scripture. They show the Word of God that has the power to pull down strongholds, bring new life and restoration.

The lampstand represents the light of the gospel shining into our world spiritually and physically. The red, white and blue of the lamp base represent the union jack - my heritage in England; the rings on the lampstand itself represent Jesus and our Father in Heaven in purple, our flesh in red, and the Holy Spirit in blue. The lamp pole is gold with a green shade to represent Australia's green and gold – where we are physically located in time at present.

Genesis 1:7

Thus God made the firmament, and divided the waters which were under the firmament from the waters which were above the firmament; and it was so.

The skyline shows the different spiritual realms that exist. It provides the viewer with a visual understanding of how far prayers can travel, not held back by time or space. We are to be inspired by God's great majesty, that He created all these things and still wants to have an intimate relationship with each of us. We are to look on in reverence to His creation but not worship creation itself.

Deuteronomy 4:19

And take heed, lest you lift your eyes to Heaven and when you see the sun, the moon, and the stars, all the host of Heaven, you feel driven to worship them and serve them, which the Lord your God has given to all the peoples under the whole heaven as a heritage. Do not worship the sun and stars.

The background shows the viewer there is more to our world than what we can currently see. There is a second and third heaven, which we have not visited but Paul writes about.

2 Corinthians 12:2

I know a man in Christ who fourteen years ago – whether in the body I do not know, or whether out of the body I do not know, God knows – such a man was caught up to the third heaven.

This scripture provides reassurance that our prayers travel across time and space to our Father in heaven. It also highlights that God wants to reveal secrets to us as our relationship with him develops.

Ask yourself the following questions:

What do God's promises mean to me?

Do I believe it? If not why not?

What does the bible say?

What actions can I take to change this mindset?

What action will I take to change this mindset?

Lightning Source UK Ltd.
Milton Keynes UK
UKHW020614300822
408056UK00005B/39

9 781922 588173